ACTIVITY WORKBOOK

SIDE by SIDE

THIRD EDITION

BOOK 2

W9-ATL-213

Steven J. Molinsky
Bill Bliss

with

Carolyn Graham • Peter S. Bliss

Contributing Authors

Dorothy Lynde • Elizabeth Handley

Illustrated by
Richard E. Hill

Longman

Side by Side, 3rd edition
Activity Workbook 2

Pearson Education, 10 Bank Street, White Plains, NY 10606

Vice president, director of publishing: *Allen Ascher*
Editorial manager: *Pam Fishman*
Vice president, director of design and production: *Rhea Banker*
Associate director of electronic production: *Aliza Greenblatt*
Production manager: *Ray Keating*
Director of manufacturing: *Patrice Fraccio*
Associate digital layout manager: *Paula D. Williams*
Digital layout specialists: *Lisa Ghiozzi, Monika Popowitz, Wendy Wolf*
Interior design: *Wendy Wolf*
Cover design: *Elizabeth Carlson*

Illustrator: *Richard E. Hill*

The authors gratefully acknowledge the contribution
of Tina Carver in the development of the original
Side by Side program.

Longman on the Web
Longman.com offers classroom activities, teaching tips and online resources for teachers of all levels and students of all ages. Visit us for course-specific Companion Websites, our comprehensive online catalogue of all Longman titles, and access to all local Longman websites, offices and contacts around the world.

Join a global community of teachers and students at **Longman.com**.

Longman English Success offers online courses to give learners flexible, self-paced study options. Developed for distance learning or to complement classroom instruction, courses over General English, Business English, and Exam Preparation.

For more information visit **EnglishSuccess.com**.

ISBN 0-13-026750-3

Printed in the United States of America

12 13 14 15 – CRK – 11 10 09 08 07 06

CONTENTS

A   WHAT DO THEY LIKE TO DO?

1

chat online	go hiking	go to the mall	play soccer	write letters
go dancing	go to the beach	listen to music	watch TV	

1. He _____likes to_____ _____watch TV_____ .

2. They _____ _____ .

3. She _____ _____ .

4. I _____ _____ .

5. They _____ _____ .

6. He _____ _____ .

7. She _____ _____ .

8. We _____ _____ .

9. My dog _____

B   LISTENING

Listen and choose the correct response.

1. a. He likes to chat online.
   b. They like to chat online.

2. a. I like to dance.
   b. She likes to dance.

3. a. He likes to read.
   b. She likes to read.

4. a. They like to play basketball.
   b. We like to play basketball.

5. a. He likes to go to the library.
   b. We like to go to the library.

6. a. You like to go to the mall.
   b. I like to go to the mall.

7. a. We like to play loud music.
   b. He likes to play loud music.

8. a. She likes to watch TV.
   b. They like to watch TV.

C WHAT DO THEY LIKE TO DO?

bake	go	listen	ride	sing	watch

1. Alan likes to _____watch_____ TV.

   _____He watches_____ TV every day.

   _____He watched_____ TV yesterday.

   _____He's going to watch_____ TV tomorrow.

2. I like to _____ to music.

   _____ to music every day.

   _____ to music yesterday.

   _____ to music tomorrow.

3. Thelma likes to _____ her bicycle.

   _____ her bicycle every day.

   _____ her bicycle yesterday.

   _____ her bicycle tomorrow.

4. My parents like to _____ .

   _____ every day.

   _____ yesterday.

   _____ tomorrow.

5. My wife and I like to _____ cookies.

   _____ cookies every day.

   _____ cookies yesterday.

   _____ cookies tomorrow.

6. Brian likes to _____ sailing.

   _____ sailing every day.

   _____ sailing yesterday.

   _____ sailing tomorrow.

D LIKES AND DISLIKES

| clean | cook | drive | eat | feed | go | read | take | wait | watch |

| like to
likes to | | don't like to
doesn't like to |

1. Ronald ___likes to cook___ spaghetti.

2. Sally ___doesn't like to take___ the subway.

3. My children _____ the birds in the park.

4. Ted and Amy _____ in noisy restaurants.

5. My wife _____ novels.

6. Arnold _____ for the bus.

7. My friends and I _____ videos.

8. I _____ downtown.

9. Howard _____ his house.

10. Tim and Jim _____ to the doctor.

What do you like to do?   **What don't you like to do?**

I like to ....   I don't like to ....

I ....   I ....

I ....   I ....

I ....   I ....

I ....   I ....

F DAY AFTER DAY

| do | get up | go | make | plant | play | study | visit | wash | write |

1. Tim _____washes_____ his car every day.

   _____He washed_____ his car yesterday.

   _____He's going to wash_____ his car tomorrow.

2. Alice _____ early every morning.

   _____ early yesterday morning.

   _____ early tomorrow morning.

3. Millie and Max _____ dancing every Friday.

   _____ dancing last Friday.

   _____ dancing next Friday.

4. I _____ English every evening.

   _____ English yesterday evening.

   _____ English tomorrow evening.

(continued)

5. The man next door _____ the drums every night.

_____ the drums last night.

_____ the drums tomorrow night.

6. My mother _____ pancakes for breakfast every Sunday.

_____ pancakes last Sunday.

_____ pancakes next Sunday.

7. My wife and I _____ flowers every spring.

_____ flowers last spring.

_____ flowers next spring.

8. Steven _____ to his girlfriend every week.

_____ to her last week.

_____ to her next week.

9. Julie _____ her grandparents every weekend.

_____ them last weekend.

_____ them next weekend.

10. My husband and I _____ yoga every afternoon.

_____ yoga yesterday afternoon.

_____ yoga tomorrow afternoon.

11. I .... every ....

....

....

GRAMMARRAP: *I Don't Like to Rush*

Listen. Then clap and practice.

I   don't like to   rush.   Do you?
I   don't like to   hurry.
I   don't like to   get   upset.
I   don't like to   worry.

I'm not   going to   rush.   Are you?
I'm not   going to   hurry.
I'm not   going to   get   upset.
I'm not   going to   worry!

GRAMMARRAP: *He Doesn't Like to Watch TV*

Listen. Then clap and practice.

He doesn't   like to   watch   TV.
He doesn't   like to   dance.
He doesn't   like to   cook or   sew
or wash or   iron his   pants.

She doesn't   like to   go to the   beach.
She doesn't   like to   shop.
She doesn't   like to   vacuum her   rugs
or dust or   wax or   mop.

Activity Workbook **7**

I WHAT'S PAULA GOING TO GIVE HER FAMILY?

Paula is looking for presents for her family.
Here's what she's going to give them.

cell phone
gloves
CD player
novel
dog
plant
watch
sweater

1. Her husband's hands are always cold. _____She's going to give him gloves._____

2. Her daughter loves animals. _____

3. Her son never arrives on time. _____

4. Her parents like to listen to music. _____

5. Her sister likes clothes. _____

6. Her brother likes to read. _____

7. Her grandparents like flowers. _____

8. Her cousin Charlie likes to talk to his friends. _____

J PRESENTS

1. Last year I ___gave___ my husband pajamas.

   This year _____I'm going to give him_____ a bathrobe.

2. Last year Bobby _____ his grandmother candy.

   This year _____ flowers.

3. Last year Carol _____ her boyfriend a tee shirt.

   This year _____ sweat pants.

4. Last year we _____ our children a bird.

   This year _____ a dog.

5. Last year I _____ my girlfriend perfume.

   This year _____ a ring.

6. Last year we _____ our son a sweater.

   This year _____ a bicycle.

7. Last year I ....

   This year ....

| he | her | him | I | me | she | they | them | us | we | you |

1. A. What did you give your wife for her birthday?

   B. _____I_____ gave _____her_____ earrings.

2. A. What did your children give you for your birthday?

   B. _____ gave _____ a book.

3. A. What did Michael give his parents for their anniversary?

   B. _____ gave _____ a CD player.

4. A. What did your friends give you and your husband for your anniversary?

   B. _____ gave _____ a plant.

5. A. What did your wife give you for your birthday?

   B. _____ gave _____ a briefcase.

6. A. What did you and your wife give your son for his birthday?

   B. _____ gave _____ a bicycle.

7. A. I forget. What did you give me for my last birthday?

   B. _____ gave _____ a painting.

8. A. I forget. What did I give you for *your* last birthday?

   B. _____ gave _____ a dress.

1st first	7th seventh	13th thirteenth	19th nineteenth	50th fiftieth
2nd second	8th eighth	14th fourteenth	20th twentieth	60th sixtieth
3rd third	9th ninth	15th fifteenth	21st twenty-first	70th seventieth
4th fourth	10th tenth	16th sixteenth	22nd twenty-second	80th eightieth
5th fifth	11th eleventh	17th seventeenth	30th thirtieth	90th ninetieth
6th sixth	12th twelfth	18th eighteenth	40th fortieth	100th one hundredth

L MATCHING

_b_ 1. eighth   **a.** 2nd   ___ 5. thirty-third   **e.** 14th

___ 2. one hundredth   **b.** 8th   ___ 6. thirteenth   **f.** 13th

___ 3. second   **c.** 20th   ___ 7. fourteenth   **g.** 40th

___ 4. twentieth   **d.** 100th   ___ 8. fortieth   **h.** 33rd

M WHAT'S THE NUMBER?

1. fiftieth   _50th_   6. first   _____

2. ninety-ninth   _____   7. sixteenth   _____

3. fifteenth   _____   8. sixty-fifth   _____

4. twelfth   _____   9. eighty-fourth   _____

5. seventy-seventh   _____   10. thirty-sixth   _____

N LISTENING

Listen and write the ordinal number you hear.

1. barber shop   _2nd_

2. Wong family   _____

3. Acme Company   _____

4. Bob Richards   _____

5. bank   _____

6. dentist's office   _____

7. flower shop   _____

8. Martinez family   _____

9. Louise Lane   _____

10. computer store   _____

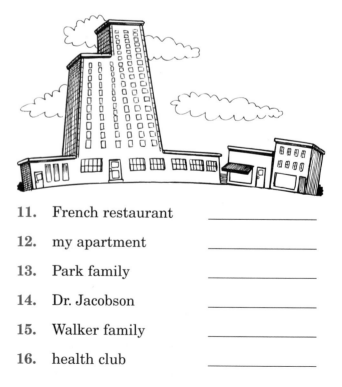

11. French restaurant   _____

12. my apartment   _____

13. Park family   _____

14. Dr. Jacobson   _____

15. Walker family   _____

16. health club   _____

O RICHARD'S BIRTHDAYS

Fill in the missing words.

On Richard's 7th birthday, he (have) __had__ [1] a party at home. His mother (make) _____ [2] pizza, and his father (bake) _____ [3] a cake. Richard's parents (give) _____ [4] him a new dog. Richard's friends (love) _____ [5] his birthday party because they (play) _____ [6] with his new dog, but Richard was upset because his mother didn't (give) _____ [7] the dog any cake to eat.

On Richard's 10th birthday, he (go) _____ [8] to the beach with his friends. They (swim) _____ [9] at the beach, and they (go) _____ [10] to a restaurant to eat. Richard's friends (like) _____ [11] his birthday party, but Richard was upset because he didn't (like) _____ [12] his present. His friends (give) _____ [13] him a wallet, but he (want) _____ [14] a baseball.

On Richard's 13th birthday, he (have) _____ [15] a picnic. His mother (cook) _____ [16] hot dogs and hamburgers. They (eat) _____ [17] delicious food and (play) _____ [18] baseball. All of his friends (enjoy) _____ [19] his birthday party, but Richard was upset because the girls didn't (talk) _____ [20] to him.

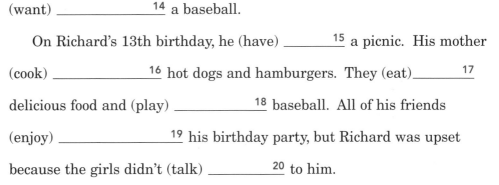

On Richard's 16th birthday, he didn't (have) _____ [21] a party. He (go) _____ [22] dancing with his girlfriend, and he (have) _____ [23] a wonderful time. His friends didn't (give) _____ [24] him presents and his parents didn't (cook) _____ [25]. But Richard wasn't upset because he (dance) _____ [26] with his girlfriend all night.

P MATCHING

__b__ **1.** Richard didn't like his present _____.

2. He went dancing _____.

3. His parents gave him a dog _____.

4. The girls didn't talk to Richard _____.

a. on his 7th birthday

b. on his 10th birthday

c. on his 13th birthday

d. on his 16th birthday

A WHAT'S THE FOOD?

apples	cheese	ice cream	meat	pepper
bread	eggs	ketchup	mustard	potatoes
cake	flour	lettuce	onions	soy sauce
carrots	grapes	mayonnaise	oranges	tomatoes

1. tomatoes

2. _____

3. _____

4. _____

5. _____

6. _____

7. _____

8. _____

9. _____

10. _____

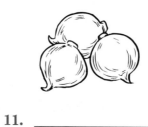

11. _____

12. _____

13. _____

14. _____

15. _____

16. _____

17. _____

18. _____

19. _____

20. _____

B WHAT ARE THEY SAYING?

Where's	Where are	It's	They're

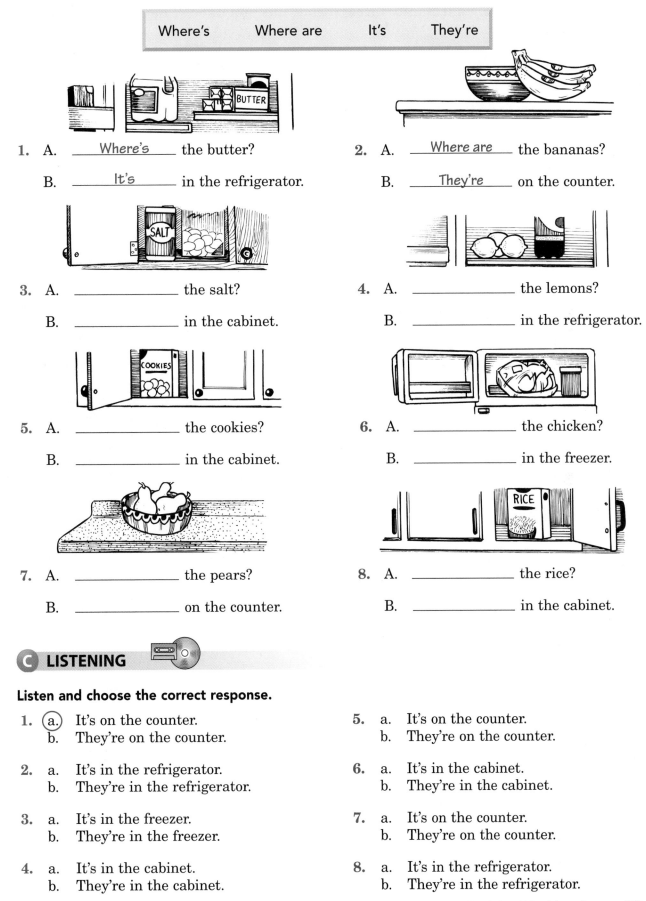

1. A. _____Where's_____ the butter?

   B. _____It's_____ in the refrigerator.

2. A. _____Where are_____ the bananas?

   B. _____They're_____ on the counter.

3. A. _____ the salt?

   B. _____ in the cabinet.

4. A. _____ the lemons?

   B. _____ in the refrigerator.

5. A. _____ the cookies?

   B. _____ in the cabinet.

6. A. _____ the chicken?

   B. _____ in the freezer.

7. A. _____ the pears?

   B. _____ on the counter.

8. A. _____ the rice?

   B. _____ in the cabinet.

C LISTENING

Listen and choose the correct response.

1. a. It's on the counter.
   b. They're on the counter.

2. a. It's in the refrigerator.
   b. They're in the refrigerator.

3. a. It's in the freezer.
   b. They're in the freezer.

4. a. It's in the cabinet.
   b. They're in the cabinet.

5. a. It's on the counter.
   b. They're on the counter.

6. a. It's in the cabinet.
   b. They're in the cabinet.

7. a. It's on the counter.
   b. They're on the counter.

8. a. It's in the refrigerator.
   b. They're in the refrigerator.

D I'M SORRY, BUT...

Look at the menu to see what Randy's Restaurant has and doesn't have today.

Today's Menu
spaghetti
hamburgers
salad
ice cream
apple pie
milk
soda

1. A. May I have a hamburger and some french fries?

   B. I'm sorry, but _____ there aren't _____

   _____ any french fries _____ .

2. A. May I please have a salad and some tea?

   B. I'm sorry, but _____ there isn't _____

   _____ any tea _____ .

3. A. May I have chicken and some milk?

   B. I'm sorry, but _____

   _____ .

4. A. May I have ice cream and some cookies?

   B. I'm sorry, but _____

   _____ .

5. A. May I have cake and some soda?

   B. I'm sorry, but _____

   _____ .

6. A. May we have two sandwiches, please?

   B. I'm sorry, but _____

   _____ .

7. A. May I have apple pie and some orange juice?

   B. I'm sorry, but _____

   _____ .

8. A. May I have spaghetti and some meatballs?

   B. I'm sorry, but _____

   _____ .

E THERE ISN'T/THERE AREN'T

1. There _____isn't any mayonnaise_____ .

   How about some _____mustard_____ ?

2. There _____aren't any bananas_____ .

   How about some _____grapes_____ ?

3. There _____ .

   How about some _____ ?

4. There _____ .

   How about some _____ ?

5. There _____ .

   How about some _____ ?

6. There _____ .

   How about some _____ ?

7. There _____ .

   How about some _____ ?

8. There _____ .

   How about some _____ ?

F LISTENING

Listen and put a check (✓) under the correct picture.

1. _____ ✔ 2. _____ _____ 3. _____ _____

4. _____ _____ 5. _____ _____ 6. _____ _____

G WHAT'S THE WORD?

how much	too much	how many	too many	a little	a few

1. A. _____How many_____ meatballs do you want?

   B. Not _____too many_____.

   Just _____a few_____.

2. A. _____How much_____ cheese do you want?

   B. Not _____too much_____.

   Just _____a little_____.

3. A. _____ ice cream do you want?

   B. Not _____.

   Just _____.

4. A. _____ cookies do you want?

   B. Not _____.

   Just _____.

5. A. _____ lemonade do you want?

   B. Not _____.

   Just _____.

6. A. _____ oranges do you want?

   B. Not _____.

   Just _____.

H WHAT'S THE PROBLEM?

too much	too many

1. She cooked _____too many_____ meatballs.

2. He drinks _____ soda.

3. They ate _____ ice cream.

4. Henry had _____ onions.

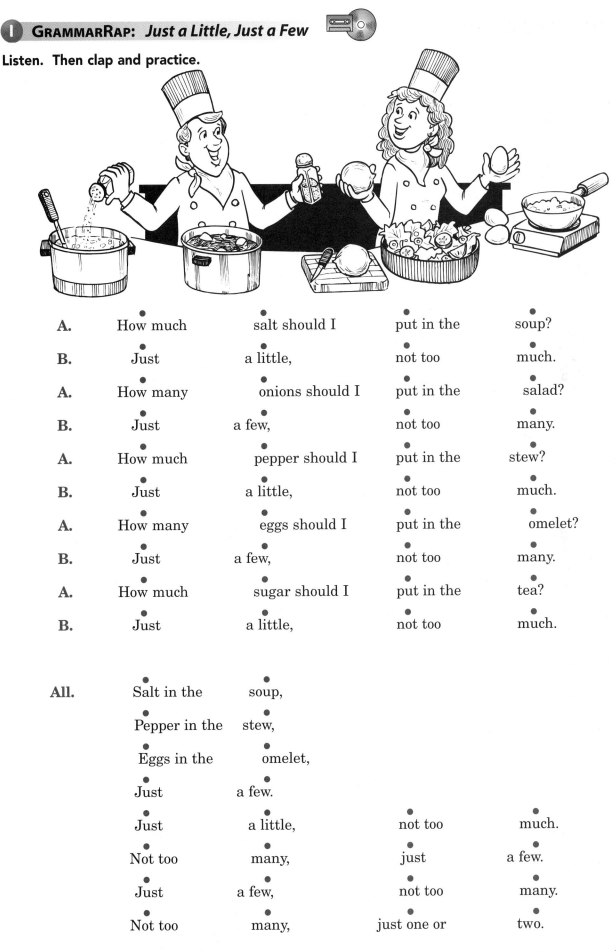

GrammarRap: *Just a Little, Just a Few*

Listen. Then clap and practice.

A.   How much   salt should I   put in the   soup?

B.   Just   a little,   not too   much.

A.   How many   onions should I   put in the   salad?

B.   Just   a few,   not too   many.

A.   How much   pepper should I   put in the   stew?

B.   Just   a little,   not too   much.

A.   How many   eggs should I   put in the   omelet?

B.   Just   a few,   not too   many.

A.   How much   sugar should I   put in the   tea?

B.   Just   a little,   not too   much.

All.   Salt in the   soup,

      Pepper in the   stew,

      Eggs in the   omelet,

      Just   a few.

      Just   a little,   not too   much.

      Not too   many,   just   a few.

      Just   a few,   not too   many.

      Not too   many,   just one or   two.

little	much	this		is	it's		it
few	many		these	are		they're	them

1. A. Would you care for some more chocolate cake?

   B. Yes, please. But only a ___little___.

   My dentist says I eat too ___much___ chocolate cake.

2. A. Would you care for some more french fries?

   B. Yes, please. But only a _____.

   My wife says I eat too _____ french fries.

3. A. _____ pizza _____ fantastic.

   B. I'm glad you like _____. Would you

   care for a _____ more?

   A. Yes, please.

4. A. _____ potatoes _____ good.

   B. I'm glad you like _____. Would you

   care for a _____ more?

   A. No, thank you.

5. A. Would you like a _____ yogurt?

   B. Yes, please. My doctor says _____ good for my health.

6. A. Would you care for some cookies? I

   baked _____ this morning.

   B. Yes, please. But just a _____.

7. A. Would you care for some more pie?

   B. Yes, please. I know _____ bad for

   my health, but I really like _____.

8. A. You're eating too _____ meatballs!

   B. I know. But _____ really good.

   Can I have just a _____ more?

K MATCHING

<u>e</u>   **1.** This pie is very good!

_____   **2.** How do you like the hamburgers?

_____   **3.** I think these cookies are excellent!

_____   **4.** How much rice do you want?

_____   **5.** Where's the tea?

_____   **6.** Let's make some lemonade!

_____   **7.** How do you like the pizza?

_____   **8.** Where are the bananas?

_____   **9.** How many carrots do you want?

_____ **10.** Let's bake a cake for dessert!

a. We can't. There isn't any flour.

b. I think it's delicious.

c. Just a little.

d. They're on the counter.

e. I'm glad you like it.

f. Just a few.

g. We can't. There aren't any lemons.

h. I'm glad you like them.

i. It's in the cabinet.

j. I think they're delicious.

L LISTENING

Listen and put a check (✓) under the correct picture.

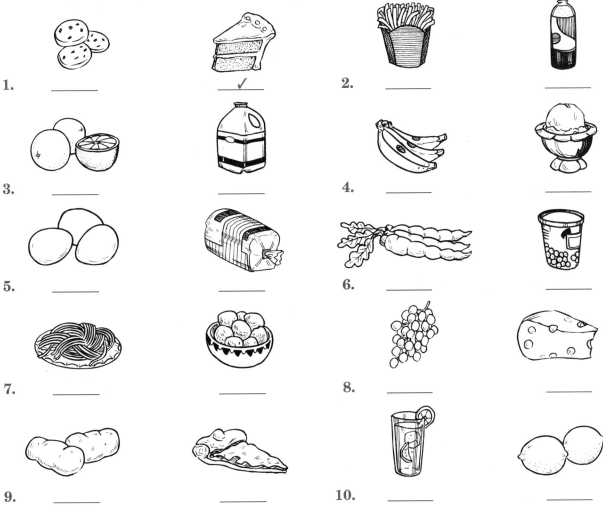

Listen. Then clap and practice.

All.   Not too   much, just   a little,

            Not too   many, just   a few.

            Not too   much, just   a little,

            Not too   many, just   a few.

A.   Would you   like more   chicken?

B.   Just   a little.

A.   Would you   like more   carrots?

B.   Just   a few.

A.   Would you   like more   gravy?

B.   Just   a little.

A.   Would you   like more   mushrooms?

B.   Just   a few.

A.   Would you   like more   salad?

B.   Just   a little.

A.   Would you   like more   tomatoes?

B.   Just   a few.

A.   Would you   like more   coffee?

B.   Just   a little.

A.   Would you   like more   cookies?

B.   Just   a few.

All.   Not too   much, just   a little.

            Not too   many, just   a few.

            Not too   much, just   a little.

            Not too   many, just   a few.

bag	bunch	can	gallon	jar	loaf/loaves
bottle	box	dozen	head	pound	of

1. Jack is going to buy food at the supermarket.

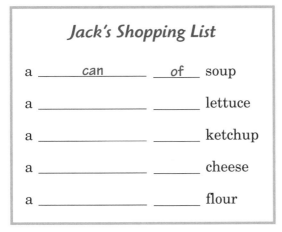

Jack's Shopping List

a _____can_____ __of__ soup

a _____ _____ lettuce

a _____ _____ ketchup

a _____ _____ cheese

a _____ _____ flour

2. Jennifer is going to make breakfast for her parents.

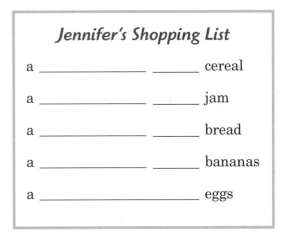

Jennifer's Shopping List

a _____ _____ cereal

a _____ _____ jam

a _____ _____ bread

a _____ _____ bananas

a _____ _____ eggs

3. Mr. and Mrs. Baxter are going to have a birthday party for their daughter.

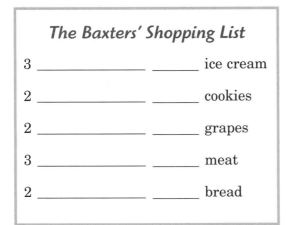

The Baxters' Shopping List

3 _____ _____ ice cream

2 _____ _____ cookies

2 _____ _____ grapes

3 _____ _____ meat

2 _____ _____ bread

4. What are YOU going to buy this week?

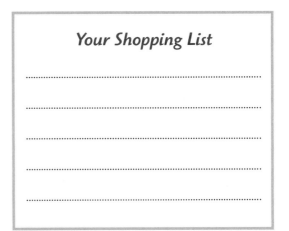

Your Shopping List

....

....

....

....

....

B WHAT ARE THEY SAYING?

| bananas | cheese | cookies | ice cream | jam | onions |

1. Do we need anything from the supermarket?

   Do we need anything else?

   Yes. We need a jar of ___jam___.

   Yes. We need a pint of _____.

2. What do we need from the supermarket?

   Do we need anything else?

   We need a bunch of _____.

   Yes. We need a box of _____.

3. Do we need anything from the supermarket?

   Do we need anything else?

   Yes. We need a bag of _____.

   Yes. We need a half a pound of _____.

C LISTENING

Listen to the conversations. Put a check (✓) under the foods you hear.

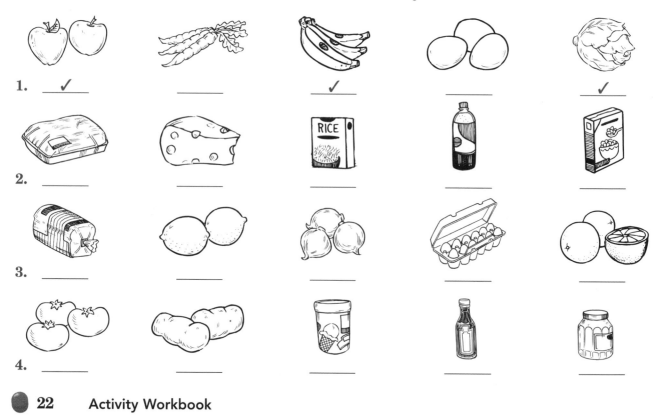

1. ___✓___   _____   ___✓___   _____   ___✓___

2. _____   _____   _____   _____   _____

3. _____   _____   _____   _____   _____

4. _____   _____   _____   _____   _____

Listen. Then clap and practice.

All. We need bread.

 Whole wheat bread.

A. How many loaves do we need?

All. Two.

All. We need beans.

 Black beans.

B. How many cans do we need?

All. Three.

All. We need rice.

 Brown rice.

C. How many pounds do we need?

All. Four.

All. We need jam.

 Strawberry jam.

D. How many jars do we need?

All. Five.

All. We need milk.

 Fresh milk.

E. How many quarts do we need?

All. Six.

All. We need cash.

 We need money.

F. How much money do we need?

All. A lot!

| are | cost | does | loaf | money | of | quart |
| bread | costs | is | loaves | much | pound | right |

1. A. How __much__ does a _____ of milk _____?

   B. A _____ of _____ _____ two thirty-nine.

   A. Two dollars and thirty-nine cents?! That's a lot of _____!

   B. You're _____. Milk _____ very expensive this week.

2. A. How _____ does a _____ _____ bread cost?

   B. A _____ of _____ _____ one twenty-nine.

   A. Good! I'll take six _____, please.

   B. Six _____?! That's a lot _____ bread!

   A. I know. But _____ _____ very cheap this week!

3. A. How _____ _____ a _____ of apples cost?

   B. A _____ _____ apples _____ three sixty-five.

   A. Three sixty five?! That's too _____ money!

   B. You're right. Apples _____ very expensive today,

   but bananas _____ very cheap.

   A. That's nice. But how can I make an apple pie with bananas?!

F LISTENING

Listen and circle the price you hear.

1.	$1.95	($1.99)	4.	$25	25¢	7.	$3.13	$3.30
2.	$5	5¢	5.	$2.74	$2.47	8.	$1.15	$1.50
3.	$4.79	$9.47	6.	$6.60	$6.16	9.	$2.10	$21

1. A. What would you like for breakfast?
   B. Please give me an order of _____.
      a. cereal
      b. (scrambled eggs)

2. A. What would you like to drink?
   B. I want a glass of _____.
      a. milk
      b. coffee

3. A. What would you like for lunch?
   B. I want a bowl of _____.
      a. pancakes
      b. soup

4. A. Would you care for some dessert?
   B. Yes. I'd like a dish of _____.
      a. ice cream
      b. hot chocolate

5. A. What would you like?
   B. Please give me a cup of _____.
      a. tea
      b. cake

6. A. What would you like for dessert?
   B. I'd like a piece of _____.
      a. strawberries
      b. apple pie

H **WHERE WOULD YOU LIKE TO GO FOR LUNCH?**

are	glass	many	order
bowl	is	much	piece
cup	it	of	they
dish			

A. Where would you like to go for lunch?

B. Let's go to Carla's Cafe. Their spaghetti ___is___¹ out of this world and _____² isn't expensive. I had an _____³ _____⁴ spaghetti there last week for a dollar ninety-five.

A. I don't really want to go to Carla's Cafe. Their spaghetti _____⁵ very good, but you can't get any chocolate milk. I like to have a _____⁶ of chocolate milk with my lunch.

B. How about The Pancake Place? Their pancakes _____⁷ fantastic, and _____⁸ aren't expensive. An _____⁹ _____¹⁰ pancakes costs two sixty-nine.

A. I really don't like The Pancake Place. The pancakes _____¹¹ tasty, but their salad _____¹² terrible! It has too _____¹³ lettuce and too _____¹⁴ onions.

B. Well, how about Rita's Restaurant? Their desserts are wonderful. You can get a delicious _____¹⁵ _____¹⁶ pie, a _____¹⁷ _____¹⁸ strawberries, or a _____¹⁹ _____²⁰ ice cream.

A. I know. But their hot chocolate _____²¹ very bad. I like to have a _____²² _____²³ hot chocolate with my dessert.

B. Wait a minute! I know where we can go for lunch. Let's go to YOUR house!

I GRAMMARRAP: *Grocery List*

Listen. Then clap and practice.

We need a loaf of	bread
And a jar of	jam,
A box of	cookies
And a pound of	ham.
A bottle of	ketchup,
A pound of	cheese,
A dozen	eggs,
And a can of	peas.
A head of	lettuce,
Half a pound of	rice,
A bunch of	bananas,
And a bag of	ice.

a loaf of bread
a jar of jam
a box of cookies
a pound of ham
a bottle of ketchup

J GRAMMARRAP: *What Would You Like to Have?*

Listen. Then clap and practice.

A. What would you like to order?
What would you like to have?

B. An order of chicken, a dish of potatoes,
A large green salad with a lot of tomatoes.
A bowl of soup, an order of rice,
And a glass of soda with a lot of ice.

A. And what would you like for dessert?

B. Nothing, thanks. I'm not very hungry!

26   Activity Workbook

K WHAT'S THE WORD?

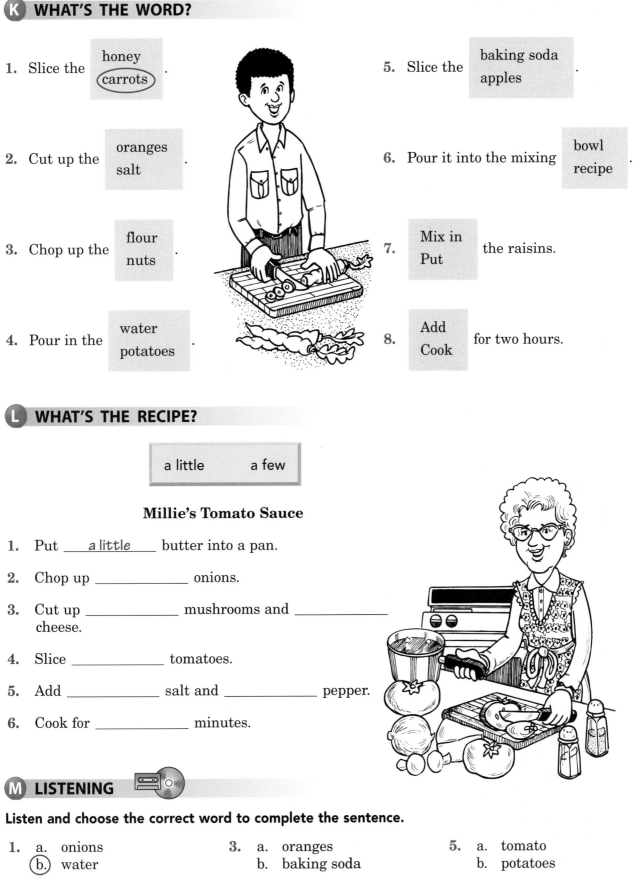

1. Slice the [honey / (carrots)] .

2. Cut up the [oranges / salt] .

3. Chop up the [flour / nuts] .

4. Pour in the [water / potatoes] .

5. Slice the [baking soda / apples] .

6. Pour it into the mixing [bowl / recipe] .

7. [Mix in / Put] the raisins.

8. [Add / Cook] for two hours.

L WHAT'S THE RECIPE?

a little	a few

Millie's Tomato Sauce

1. Put ___a little___ butter into a pan.

2. Chop up _____ onions.

3. Cut up _____ mushrooms and _____ cheese.

4. Slice _____ tomatoes.

5. Add _____ salt and _____ pepper.

6. Cook for _____ minutes.

M LISTENING

Listen and choose the correct word to complete the sentence.

1. a. onions
   b. water *(circled)*

2. a. cheese
   b. nuts

3. a. oranges
   b. baking soda

4. a. salt
   b. raisins

5. a. tomato
   b. potatoes

6. a. pepper
   b. mushrooms

✔ CHECK-UP TEST: Chapters 1-3

A. Fill in the blanks.

Ex. a ____quart____ of milk

1. a _____ of bananas

2. a _____ of soup

3. a _____ of onions

4. a _____ of pie

5. 2 _____ of cereal

6. 2 _____ of bread

B. Circle the correct answers.

Ex. Yogurt ⟨is⟩ / are cheap today.

1. I eat too much / many cookies.

2. She ate so much / many cake that

   she has a stomachache.

3. What do you like / like to do on the

   weekend?

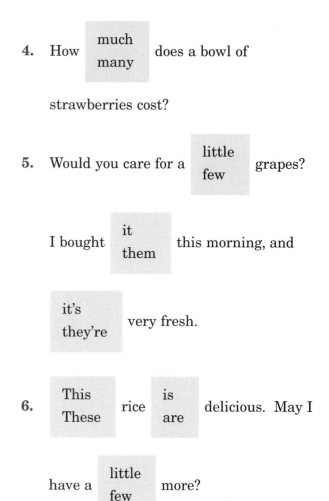

4. How much / many does a bowl of

strawberries cost?

5. Would you care for a little / few grapes?

I bought it / them this morning, and

it's / they're very fresh.

6. This / These rice is / are delicious. May I

have a little / few more?

C. Complete the sentences.

Ex. Janet watches TV every Friday.

   __She watched__ TV last Friday.

   __She's going to watch__ TV next Friday.

1. Alan drives to the mall every week.

   He _____ to the mall last week.

   _____

   to the mall next week.

2. I go on vacation every year.

   I _____ on vacation last year.

   _____

   on vacation next year.

3. We play baseball every Saturday.

   We _____ baseball last Saturday.

   _____ baseball next Saturday.

4. My sister writes letters to her friends every weekend.

   She _____ letters to her friends last weekend.

   _____ letters to her friends next weekend.

5. Ed makes pancakes every morning.

   He _____ pancakes yesterday morning.

   _____ pancakes tomorrow morning.

D. Complete the sentences.

Ex. Last year my parents gave me a sweater for my birthday.

   This year ___they're going to give me___ a jacket.

1. Last year Tom gave his girlfriend flowers.

   This year _____

   _____ candy.

2. Last year Sue gave her husband a CD player.

   This year _____

   _____ a briefcase.

3. Last year we gave our parents a cell phone.

   This year _____

   _____ a computer.

"I'm sorry, but there _____ any."

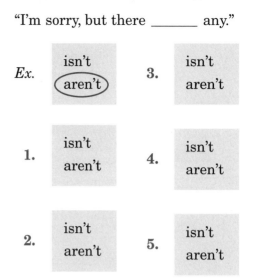

Ex. isn't (aren't)

3. isn't aren't

1. isn't aren't

4. isn't aren't

2. isn't aren't

5. isn't aren't

1. A. Will you be back soon?

    B. Yes, _____I will_____ . _____I'll_____

    _____be back_____ in half an hour.

2. A. Will the game begin soon?

    B. Yes, _____ . _____

    _____ in ten minutes.

3. A. Will Henry return soon?

    B. Yes, _____ . _____

    _____ in a week.

4. A. Will we be ready soon?

    B. Yes, _____ . _____

    _____ in a little while.

5. A. Will Grandma and Grandpa arrive soon?

    B. Yes, _____ . _____

    _____ in 15 or 20 minutes.

6. A. Will the storm end soon?

    B. Yes, _____ . _____

    _____ in a few hours.

7. A. Will Kate be here soon?

    B. Yes, _____ . _____

    _____ in a few minutes.

8. A. Will you get out soon?

    B. Yes, _____ . _____

    _____ in a month.

1. Do you think Barbara _____will_____ move to a new apartment soon?

   I don't know. Maybe _____she_____ _____will_____, and maybe _____she_____ _____won't_____.

2. Do you think Robert _____ like his new job?

   I don't know. Maybe _____, and maybe _____.

3. Do you think _____ drive to the beach this weekend?

   I don't know. Maybe I _____, and maybe _____.

4. Do you think _____ be a famous scientist some day?

   I don't know. Maybe you _____, and maybe _____.

5. Do you think _____ snow a lot this winter?

   I don't know. Maybe _____ _____, and maybe _____.

6. Do you think _____ _____ be a lot of traffic today?

   I don't know. Maybe _____, and maybe _____ _____.

7. Do you think you and Roger _____ get married soon?

   I don't know. Maybe _____, and maybe _____.

8. Do you think the guests _____ like the fruitcake?

   I don't know. Maybe _____ _____, and maybe _____.

C WHAT DO YOU THINK?

		Yes!	**No!**
1.	What will Charlie bake for the party?	Maybe ____he'll____ ____bake____ cookies.	I'm sure ____he____ ____won't bake____ a cake.
2.	What will Mom order at the restaurant?	Maybe _____ _____ a sandwich.	I'm sure _____ _____ a pizza.
3.	Where will your parents go this evening?	Maybe _____ _____ to a movie.	I'm sure _____ _____ to a party.
4.	What will you get for your birthday?	Maybe _____ _____ a sweater.	I'm sure _____ _____ a cell phone.
5.	When will the train arrive?	Maybe _____ _____ in an hour.	I'm sure _____ _____ on time.
6.	When will we finish our English book?	Maybe _____ _____ it in a few months.	I'm sure _____ _____ it next week.

D LISTENING

Listen and circle the words you hear.

1.	won't / (want to)	3.	won't / want to	5.	won't / want to	7.	won't / want to
2.	won't / want to	4.	won't / want to	6.	won't / want to	8.	won't / want to

E DIFFERENT OPINIONS

1. I think the weather will be nice tomorrow. Everybody else thinks ____it 'll be____ bad.

2. My wife thinks the guests will arrive on time. I think _____ late.

3. I think our daughter will be a lawyer. My husband thinks _____ an architect.

4. My parents think my brother Bob will buy a bicycle. I think _____ a motorcycle.

5. I think we'll have a good time at the party. My husband thinks _____ a terrible time.

F **GRAMMARRAP:** *You'll See*

Listen. Then clap and practice.

A.   I'll   remember.

B.   Are you   sure?

A.   Don't   worry.   I'll remember.   You'll see.

A.   He'll   do it.

B.   Are you   sure?

A.   Don't   worry.   He'll do it.   You'll see.

A.   She'll   call you.

B.   Are you   sure?

A.   Don't   worry.   She'll call you. You'll see.

A.   It'll be   ready.

B.   Are you   sure?

A.   Don't   worry.   It'll be ready.   You'll see.

A.   We'll   be there.

B.   Are you   sure?

A.   Don't   worry.   We'll be there.   You'll see.

A.   They'll   get there.

B.   Are you   sure?

A.   Don't   worry.   They'll get there. You'll see.

1. A. What's Bruno going to make for breakfast this morning?

    B. _____He might make eggs_____, or

    _____he might make pancakes_____.

2. A. What time is Sally going to get up tomorrow morning on her day off?

    B. _____, or

    _____.

3. A. When are your children going to clean their bedroom?

    B. _____, or

    _____.

4. A. What are you going to give your parents for their anniversary?

    B. _____, or

    _____.

5. A. What are you and your friends going to watch on TV tonight?

    B. _____, or

    _____.

6. A. Where are Mr. and Mrs. Martinez going to go for their vacation?

    B. _____, or

    _____.

7. A. Tell me, what are you going to do this weekend?

    B. _____, or

    _____.

8. A. What's Arthur going to name his new cat?

    B. _____, or

    _____.

H BE CAREFUL!

1. Don't stand there!
   - (a.) You might get hit.
   - b. You might watch.

2. Put on your safety glasses!
   - a. You might hurt your ears.
   - b. You might hurt your eyes.

3. Don't touch those wires!
   - a. You might get a shock.
   - b. You might get cold.

4. Don't touch that machine!
   - a. You might get hurt.
   - b. You might get a helmet.

5. Watch your step!
   - a. You might finish.
   - b. You might fall.

6. Put on your helmet!
   - a. You might hurt your back.
   - b. You might hurt your head.

I LOUD AND CLEAR   W!

| winter   Wendy   walk   weather   work |

1. ___Wendy___ doesn't like to ___walk___ to ___work___ in the ___winter___ when the ___weather___ is bad.

| wet   walk   waiter   won't   waitress |

2. The _____ and the _____ _____ _____ there. The floor is _____!

| wife   wash   Walter   windows   want   weekend |

3. _____ and his _____ _____ to _____ their _____ this _____.

| wasn't   we   water   wanted   warm |

4. _____ _____ to go swimming, but the _____ _____ _____.

Activity Workbook   **35**

break her leg	fall asleep	get fat	have a terrible time	rain
catch a cold	get a backache	get seasick	look terrible	step on her feet
drown	get a sunburn	get sick	miss our bus	

1. Jennifer won't go skating because

_____ she's afraid she might _____

_____ break her leg _____ .

2. George won't go to the beach because

_____

_____ .

3. I won't go swimming because

_____

_____ .

4. We won't have lunch with you because

_____

_____ .

5. My mother and father won't go on the roller

coaster because _____

_____ .

6. Brian won't go dancing with Brenda

because _____

_____ .

7. We won't go to a play because

_____

_____ .

8. I won't go to Patty's party because

_____

_____ .

9. Barry won't carry those boxes because

_____

_____ .

10. Sally won't go sailing because

_____

_____ .

11. I won't eat dessert because

_____

_____ .

12. Helen won't take a walk in the park because

_____

_____ .

13. We won't wash our clothes today because

_____

_____ .

14. Fred won't get a short haircut because

_____

_____ .

K LISTENING

Listen and choose the correct answer.

1. a. He doesn't want to go on the roller coaster.
   b. He doesn't want to go to the doctor.

2. a. She doesn't want to go skiing.
   b. She doesn't want to go to the movies.

3. a. He doesn't want to go to a play.
   b. He doesn't want to go dancing.

4. a. She doesn't want to go skiing.
   b. She doesn't want to stay home.

5. a. He doesn't want to read a book.
   b. He doesn't want to take a walk in the park.

6. a. He doesn't want to go swimming.
   b. He doesn't want to go dancing.

7. a. She doesn't want to go skating.
   b. She doesn't want to go sailing.

8. a. He doesn't want to go to the library.
   b. He doesn't want to go to the beach.

9. a. She doesn't want to go to the party.
   b. She doesn't want to eat dinner.

10. a. He doesn't want to get a short haircut.
    b. He doesn't want to buy a small dog.

Listen. Then clap and practice.

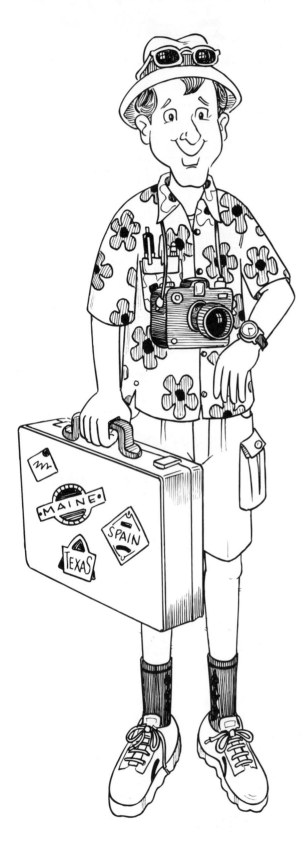

A.   When is he going to   leave?

B.   He might leave at   noon.

C.   He might leave on   Monday.

D.   He might leave in   June.

A.   Where is he going to   go?

B.   He might go to   Spain.

C.   He might go to   Texas.

D.   He might go to   Maine.

A.   How is he going to   get there?

B.   He might go by   train.

C.   He might take the   bus.

D.   He might take a   plane.

A.   Who is he going to   go with?

B.   He might go with   Ed.

C.   He might go with   Peter.

D.   He might go with   Fred.

A.   What's he going to   do there?

B.   He might see the   zoo.

C.   He might take some   pictures.

D.   He might write to   you.

Listen and fill in the words to the song. Then listen again and sing along.

cake	decide	go	her	make	Mexico	sweater	wide

I want to cook some dinner.

I don't know what to ___make___ [1].

I might make stew. I might make eggs.

I might just bake a _____ [2].

I really don't know what to cook.

The choices are so _____ [3].

I might cook this. I might cook that.

I really can't _____ [4].

I'm planning my vacation.

I don't know where to _____ [5].

I might see France. I might see Spain.

I might see _____ [6].

I really don't know where to go.

The choices are so _____ [7].

I might go here. I might go there.

I really can't _____ [8].

I'm buying Mom a present.

I don't know what to get _____ [9].

I might buy gloves. I might buy boots.

I might get her a _____ [10].

I really don't know what to get.

The choices are so _____ [11].

I might get this. I might get that.

I really can't _____ [12].

A OLD AND NEW

1. Henry's old sofa was soft. His new sofa is _____ softer _____ .

2. Nancy's old briefcase was light. Her new briefcase is _____ .

3. Bob's old living room was large. His new living room is _____ .

4. My old recipe for chili was hot. My new recipe is _____ .

5. My old boss was friendly. My new boss is _____ .

6. Our old neighborhood was safe. Our new neighborhood is _____ .

7. Linda's old cell phone was small. Her new cell phone is _____ .

8. Grandpa's old sports car was fancy. His new sports car is _____ .

9. Cathy's old mittens were warm. Her new mittens are _____ .

10. Billy's old school was big. His new school is _____ .

11. My old job was easy. My new job is _____ .

12. Our old neighbors were nice. Our new neighbors are _____ .

13. Richard's old watch was cheap. His new watch is _____ .

14. Dr. Green's old office was ugly. His new office is _____ .

B WHAT'S THE WORD?

1. A. Is Tim's hair short?

    B. Yes, but Jim's hair is _____ shorter _____ .

2. A. Is Charlie's cat cute?

    B. Yes, but his dog is _____ .

3. A. Is Debbie's dog fat?

    B. Yes, but her cat is _____ .

4. A. Is Barbara busy?

    B. Yes, but Betty is _____ .

40   Activity Workbook

C THEY'RE DIFFERENT

1. Paul's parrot is talkative, but Paula's parrot is _____more talkative_____.

2. Your roommate is interesting, but my roommate is _____.

3. Sam's suit is attractive, but Stanley's suit is _____.

4. Shirley's shoes are comfortable, but her sister's shoes are _____.

5. George is intelligent, but his brother is _____.

6. My daughter's hair is long, but my son's hair is _____.

7. Last winter was cold, but this winter is _____.

8. William is thin, but his father is _____.

9. My children are healthy, but my doctor's children are _____.

10. John's computer is powerful, but Jane's computer is _____.

11. Barbara's boyfriend is handsome, but her father is _____.

12. My teeth are white, but my dentist's teeth are _____.

13. Our neighbor's yard is beautiful, but our yard is _____.

D WHAT'S THE WORD?

1. A. This meatloaf is delicious.
   B. It's very good, but my mother's meatloaf

   is _____more delicious_____.

2. A. Chicken is good for you.
   B. I know. But everybody says that fish

   is _____ for you.

3. A. This necklace is very expensive.
   B. You're right. But that necklace

   is _____.

4. A. You're very energetic!
   B. Yes, I am. But my wife is _____

   _____.

Across

4. My upstairs neighbor is friendly, but my downstairs neighbor is _____.
7. Their baby is cute, but my baby is _____.
8. Betty's blue dress is pretty, but her green dress is _____.
11. This bicycle is fast, but that bicycle is _____.
12. My old apartment was large, but my new apartment is _____.
13. Your dishwasher is quiet, but my dishwasher is _____.

Down

1. Our old rug was soft, but our new rug is _____.
2. Yesterday it was warm, but today it's _____.
3. Their new house is small, but their old house was _____.
4. Tom's new tie is fancy, but his son's tie is _____.
5. My old tennis racket was light, but my new tennis racket is_____.
6. Bananas were cheap last week, but this week they're _____.
9. The chili we ate last week was hot, but this chili is _____.
10. This picture is ugly, but that picture is _____.

F LISTENING

Listen and choose the correct words to complete the sentences.

1. a. cooler
   b. cuter

2. a. smaller
   b. taller

3. a. more handsome
   b. more attractive

4. a. nicer
   b. lighter

5. a. fatter
   b. faster

6. a. friendlier
   b. fancier

7. a. more interesting
   b. more intelligent

8. a. bigger
   b. busier

LET'S COMPARE!

cheap	delicious	fancy	small	talented	talkative

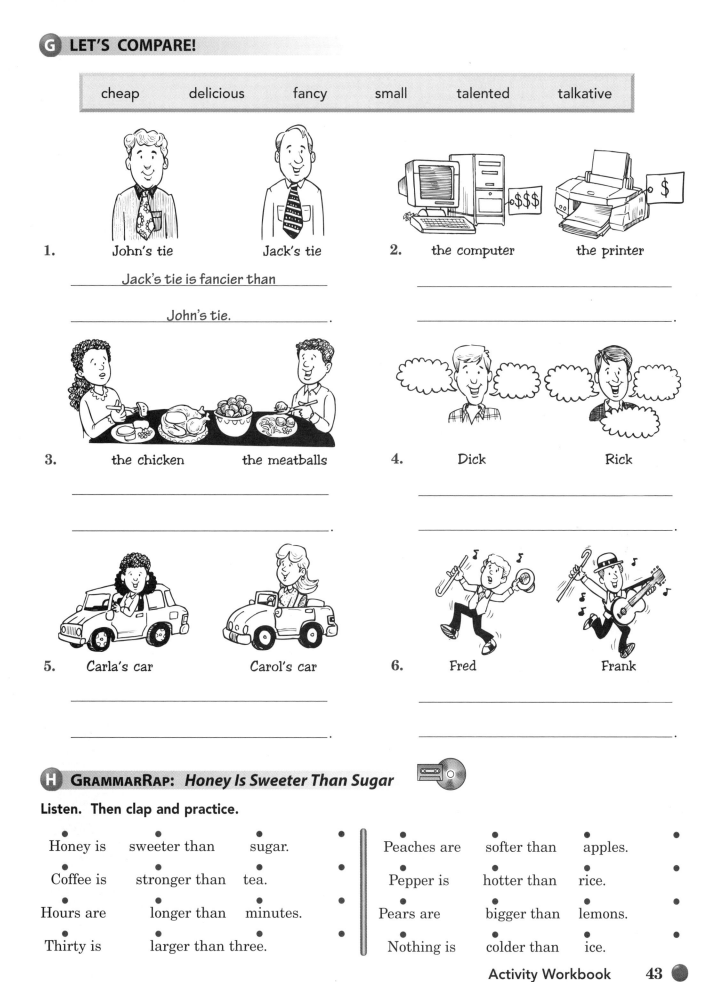

1. John's tie   Jack's tie

_____Jack's tie is fancier than_____

_____John's tie._____.

2. the computer   the printer

_____

_____.

3. the chicken   the meatballs

_____

_____.

4. Dick   Rick

_____

_____.

5. Carla's car   Carol's car

_____

_____.

6. Fred   Frank

_____

_____.

H **GRAMMARRAP:** *Honey Is Sweeter Than Sugar*

Listen. Then clap and practice.

Honey is   sweeter than   sugar.

Coffee is   stronger than   tea.

Hours are   longer than   minutes.

Thirty is   larger than three.

Peaches are   softer than   apples.

Pepper is   hotter than   rice.

Pears are   bigger than   lemons.

Nothing is   colder than   ice.

Listen and circle the correct answer.

1. yesterday   (Yes) / No   today

2. $2.50   Yes / No $3.25

3. Betty   Yes / No   Jane

4. Bob   Yes / No   Bill

5. Barry   Yes / No   Larry

6. science test   Yes / No   history test

7. Irene   Yes / No   Eileen

8. Ronald   Yes / No   Donald

J **GRAMMARRAP:** *I Can't Decide*

Listen. Then clap and practice.

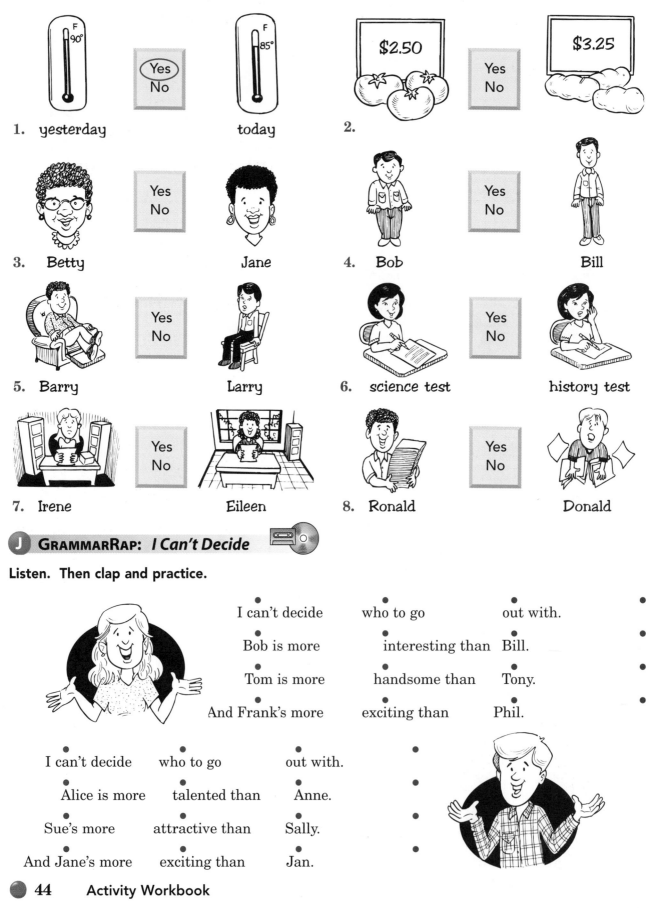

I can't decide   who to go   out with.
Bob is more   interesting than Bill.
Tom is more   handsome than   Tony.
And Frank's more   exciting than   Phil.

I can't decide   who to go   out with.
Alice is more   talented than   Anne.
Sue's more   attractive than   Sally.
And Jane's more   exciting than   Jan.

K WHAT SHOULD THEY DO?

| call the dentist | fire him | rent a video |
| call the police | hire her | plant some flowers |

1. My garden looks terrible!

   You should plant some flowers.

2. Harvey has a very bad toothache!

   _____

3. My husband and I want to see a movie tonight.

   _____

4. A thief stole my daughter's new bicycle!

   _____

5. The people at the Ace company think that Jennifer is capable and talented.

   _____

6. Ms. Hunter is upset because her secretary falls asleep at work every day.

   _____

L GRAMMARRAP: *Should They...?*

Listen. Then clap and practice.

A. Should he   call or should he   write?

B.   He should call   tomorrow   night.

A. Should I   keep it or give it   back?

B.   You should wear it or give it to   Jack.

A. Should I   stay or   should I   go?

B.   Don't ask me.   I don't   know.

Activity Workbook   45

1. Should I buy a van or a sports car?

   I think _____you should buy a van_____

   because _____vans are more useful than_____ *(or)*

   _____sports cars_____ .

   I think _____you should buy a sports car_____

   because _____sports cars are more_____

   _____exciting than vans_____ .

2. Should she buy a bicycle or a motorcycle?

   I think _____

   because _____

   _____ .

3. Should we move to Weston or Easton?

   I think _____

   because _____

   _____ .

4. Should he buy the fur hat or the leather hat?

   I think _____

   because _____

   _____ .

5. Should I vote for Alan Lane or George Gray?

   I think _____

   because _____

   _____ .

6. Should we hire Mr. Hall or Mr. Hill?

   I think _____

   because _____

   _____ .

7. Should he go out with Patty or Pam?

   I think _____

   because _____

   _____ .

N WHAT'S THE WORD?

mine	his	hers	ours	yours	theirs

1. A. Is this Michael's cell phone?

   B. No. It isn't _____his_____.

2. A. Are these your safety glasses?

   B. No. They aren't _____.

3. A. Is this your sister's violin?

   B. No. It isn't _____.

4. A. Is that Mr. and Mrs. Garcia's van?

   B. No. It isn't _____.

5. A. Is this my recipe for fruitcake?

   B. No. It isn't _____.

6. A. Are these your son's sneakers?

   B. No. They aren't _____.

7. Is that your car?

   No. It isn't _____.

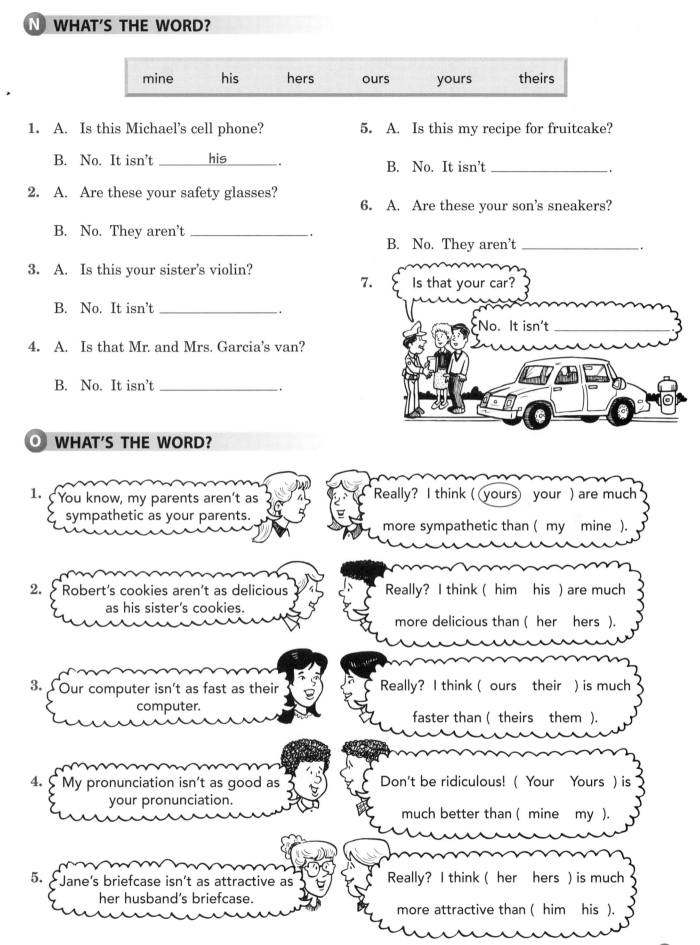

O WHAT'S THE WORD?

1. You know, my parents aren't as sympathetic as your parents.

   Really? I think ((yours) your) are much more sympathetic than (my   mine).

2. Robert's cookies aren't as delicious as his sister's cookies.

   Really? I think (him   his) are much more delicious than (her   hers).

3. Our computer isn't as fast as their computer.

   Really? I think (ours   their) is much faster than (theirs   them).

4. My pronunciation isn't as good as your pronunciation.

   Don't be ridiculous! (Your   Yours) is much better than (mine   my).

5. Jane's briefcase isn't as attractive as her husband's briefcase.

   Really? I think (her   hers) is much more attractive than (him   his).

P DIFFERENT, BUT OKAY

1. My neighborhood (quiet) _____ isn't as quiet as _____ your neighborhood, but it's much (interesting) _____ more interesting _____ .

2. Susan's sofa (fashionable) _____ her sister's sofa, but it's much (comfortable) _____ .

3. These apartments (modern) _____ our apartment, but they're much (large) _____ .

4. George's car (powerful) _____ Jack's car, but it's much (reliable) _____ .

5. The weather in our city (warm) _____ the weather in your city, but it's much (sunny) _____ .

6. My parents (talkative) _____ my cousin's parents, but they're much (understanding) _____ .

7. The movie we rented last weekend wasn't (exciting) _____ this movie, but it was much (good) _____ .

Q YOU'RE RIGHT

1. A. Ken's tie isn't as attractive as Len's tie.
   B. You're right. Len's tie is _____ more _____
   _____ attractive than Ken's tie _____ .

2. A. Donald isn't as nice as Ronald.
   B. You're right. Ronald is _____
   _____ .

3. A. Larry isn't as lazy as his brother.
   B. You're right. Larry's brother is _____
   _____ .

4. A. English isn't as difficult as Russian.
   B. You're right. Russian is _____
   _____ .

5. A. Julie's office isn't as big as Judy's office.
   B. You're right. Judy's office is _____
   _____ .

6. A. My son isn't as talkative as your son.
   B. You're right. My son is _____
   _____ .

Listen. Then clap and practice.

Where's my	ticket?
Who has	mine?
I don't	want to
stand in	line.
Who has	hers?
Who has	his?
I wonder	where
my ticket	is!
He has	his.
I have	mine.
She has	hers.
Everything's	fine!

S GRAMMARRAP: *His Job Is Easy*

Listen. Then clap and practice.

His job is	easy.		
Hers is,	too.		
Mine's a more	difficult	job to	do.
His job's as	simple		
As A B	C.		
Mine	requires a	P h	D.

T WHO SHOULD WE HIRE?

A. Do you think we should hire Mr. Blake or Mr. Maxwell?

B. I'm not sure. Mr. Blake isn't as (lively) _____lively_____ ¹

as Mr. Maxwell, but he's much (smart) _____ ².

A. I agree. Mr. Blake is very smart, but in my opinion,

Mr. Maxwell is (talented) _____ ³ than
Mr. Blake.

B. Well, perhaps Mr. Blake isn't as (talented) _____ ⁴ as

Mr. Maxwell, but I think he's probably (honest) _____ ⁵.

A. Do you really think so?

B. Yes. I think Mr. Blake is much (good) _____ ⁶ for the job.
We should hire him.

A. Do you think we should hire Ms. Taylor or Ms. Tyler?

B. I'm not sure. Ms. Tyler isn't as (friendly) _____ ⁷

as Ms. Taylor, but I think she's much (intelligent) _____

_____ ⁸.

A. But Ms. Taylor is (talkative) _____ ⁹

and (polite) _____ ¹⁰ than Ms. Tyler.

B. That's true. But I think Ms. Tyler is (capable) _____

_____ ¹¹ than Ms. Taylor. I think we should hire her.

A. Do you think we should hire Mario or Victor?

B. I don't know. Mario's meatballs are (good) _____ ¹²

than Victor's, but his desserts aren't as (delicious)

_____ ¹³ as Victor's desserts.

A. That's true. But Mario's vegetable stew is (interesting)

_____ ¹⁴ than Victor's. Also, Mario is

much (fast) _____ ¹⁵ than Victor. He's also

(nice) _____ ¹⁶ than Victor.

B. You're right. I think we should hire Mario.

1. A. I think Alice is very bright.

    B. She certainly is. She's ___the___

    ___brightest___ student in our class.

2. A. Your brother Tom is very neat.

    B. He certainly is. He's _____

    _____ person I know.

3. A. Our upstairs neighbors are very nice.

    B. I agree. They're _____
        people in the building.

4. A. This dress is very fancy.

    B. I know. It's _____
        dress in the store.

5. A. I think Nancy is very friendly.

    B. I agree. She's _____
        person in our office.

6. A. Timothy is very quiet.

    B. I know. He's _____
        boy in the school.

7. A. Is their new baby cute?

    B. In my opinion, she's _____

    _____ baby girl in
        the hospital.

8. A. That dog is very big.

    B. It certainly is. It's _____

    _____ dog in the
        neighborhood.

9. A. Your cousin Steven is very sloppy.

    B. He certainly is. He's _____

    _____ person I know.

10. A. Morton Miller is very mean.

    B. I agree. He's _____

    _____ man in town.

boring ∨	generous ∨	interesting ∨	patient	smart ∨	talented ∨
energetic ∨	honest	noisy	polite ∨	stubborn ∨	

1. Jessica sings, dances, and plays the guitar. She's very _____talented_____.

   In fact, she's _____the most talented_____ person I know.

2. Mr. Bates gives very expensive gifts to his friends. He's very _____.

   In fact, he's _____ person I know.

3. My Aunt Louise jogs every day before work. She's very _____.

   In fact, she's _____ person I know.

4. Marvin always says "Thank you" and "You're welcome." He's very _____.

   In fact, he's _____ person I know.

5. Samantha always knows the answers to all the questions. She's very _____.

   In fact, she's _____ person I know.

6. Edward isn't reading a very exciting novel. It's very _____.

   In fact, it's _____ book in his house.

7. Dr. Chen never gets angry. She's very _____.

   In fact, she's _____ person I know.

8. Mayor Jones always says what he thinks. He's very _____.

   In fact, he's _____ person I know.

9. My next-door neighbor plays loud music after midnight. He's very _____.

   In fact, he's _____ person I know.

10. I'm never bored in my English class. My English teacher is very _____.

    In fact, she's _____ person I know.

11. My brother-in-law is always sure he's right. He's very _____.

    In fact, he's _____ person I know.

WorldBuy.com is a very popular website on the Internet. People like to shop there because they can find wonderful products from around the world at very low prices.

1. *(attractive!)* Julie is buying a briefcase from Italy because she thinks that Italian briefcases are _____ the most attractive _____ briefcases in the world.

2. *(soft!)* David is buying leather boots from Spain because he thinks that Spanish boots are _____ boots in the world.

3. *(elegant!)* Francine is buying an evening gown from Paris because she thinks that French evening gowns are _____ gowns in the world.

4. *(modern!)* Mr. and Mrs. Chang are buying a sofa from Sweden because they think that Swedish furniture is _____ furniture in the world.

5. *(warm!)* Victor is buying a fur hat from Russia because he thinks that Russian hats are _____ hats in the world.

6. *(good!)* Brenda is buying a sweater from England because she thinks that English sweaters are _____ sweaters in the world.

7. *(reliable!)* Michael is buying a watch from Switzerland because he thinks that Swiss watches are _____ watches in the world.

8. *(beautiful!)* Mr. and Mrs. Rivera are buying a rug from China because they think that Chinese rugs are _____ rugs in the world.

9. *(delicious!)* Nancy is buying coffee from Brazil because she thinks that Brazilian coffee is _____ in the world.

10. *(................!)* I'm buying .... from .... because I think that ....s is/are .... in the world.

D GRAMMARRAP: *What Do You Think About . . . ?*

Listen. Then clap and practice.

A.   What do you   think about   Kirk?

B.   He's the friendliest   person at   work!

A.   What do you   think about   Flo?

B.   She's the most patient   person I   know!

A.   What do you   think about   Pete?

B.   He's the nicest   boy on the   street!

A.   What do you   think about   Kate?

B. She's the most talented   teacher in the   state!

A.   What do you   think about   Bob?

B.   He's the laziest   guy on the   job!

A.   What do you   think about   Frank?

B. He's the most polite   teller at the   bank!

A.   What do you   think about   Nellie?

B.   She's the fastest   waitress at the   deli!

A.   What do you   think about this   kitty?

B.   It's the ugliest   cat in the   city!

1. A. How do you like your new BMB van, Mr. Lopez?

    B. It's very powerful. It's much ___more___

    _____powerful_____ than my old van.

    A. That's because the BMB van is _____

    ___the most powerful___ van in the world!

2. A. How do you like your Suny video camera, Mrs. Park?

    B. It's very lightweight. It's much _____

    _____ than my old video camera.

    A. That's because the Suny video camera is _____

    _____ video camera in the world!

3. A. How do you like your new Inkflo printer, Ted?

    B. It's very efficient. It's much _____

    _____ than my old printer.

    A. That's because the Inkflo printer is _____

    _____ printer in the world!

4. A. How do you like your Panorama fax machine, Jane?

    B. It's very dependable. It's much _____

    _____ than my old fax machine.

    A. That's because the Panorama fax machine is _____

    _____ fax machine in the world!

5. A. How do you like your new Ever-Lite Flashlight, Henry?

    B. It's very bright. It's much _____ than the flashlight I usually use.

    A. That's because the Ever-Lite Flashlight is _____

    _____ flashlight in the world!

Listen and circle the words you hear.

1. (more comfortable)   the most comfortable
2. the best   the worst
3. more energetic   the most energetic
4. cheap   cheaper
5. the most important   more important

6. sloppier   the sloppiest
7. the worst   the best
8. lazier   lazy
9. meaner   mean
10. more honest   the most honest

G PUZZLE

| boring   comfortable   delicious   good   honest   polite   safe   sloppy   small   ugly |

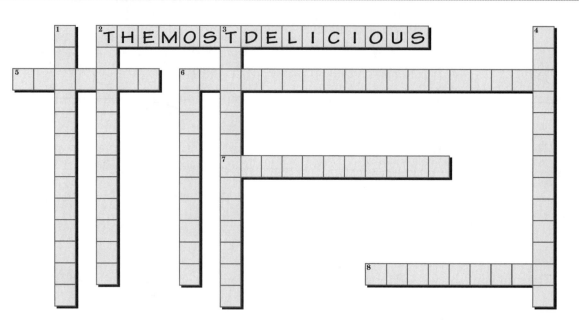

Across

2. Some people don't like this cereal. But I disagree. I think it's _____ cereal in the world.

5. Even though Harry's Restaurant is the most popular restaurant in town, it isn't _____.

6. This is my favorite chair. That's because it's _____ chair in the house.

7. My house isn't very big. In fact, it's _____ house on the street.

8. Their old neighborhood was dangerous, but their new neighborhood is _____ neighborhood in the city.

Down

1. Even though the salespeople at Ace Used Cars are the most helpful in town, they aren't _____.

2. My son isn't very neat. In my opinion, he's _____ person in our family.

3. I think golf is very interesting. But my wife disagrees. She thinks it's _____ game in the world.

4. Charles is never rude. In fact, he's _____ boy in the school.

6. Emily's cat isn't very pretty. In my opinion, it's _____ cat in town!

Fill in the words. Then read the sentences aloud.

worst	program	Andrew
terrible		actor

1. <u>   Andrew   </u> is the <u>   worst   </u>

   <u>   actor   </u> on this <u>   terrible   </u>

   TV <u>   program   </u>!

recipe	Carla's	fruitcake
recommend		better

2. I _____ _____

   _____ for _____.

   It's _____ than yours.

energetic	friendlier	Robert
more		brother

3. _____ is _____

   and _____ _____

   than his _____ Richard.

newspaper	writes	reads
Rita		morning

4. _____ _____ the _____

   every _____, and she

   _____ letters every afternoon.

perfume	birthday	sister
Ronald		thirtieth

5. _____ gave his _____

   flowers and _____ for her

   _____ _____.

powerful	bigger	more
neighbor's		car

6. My _____ is _____ and

   _____ _____ than my

   _____ car.

A. Complete the sentences.

Ex. Will you be ready soon?

Yes, __I will__. ___I'll___
be ready in a few minutes.

Ex. Will your brother get home soon?

No, __he won't__. He's at a baseball
game tonight.

1. Will the storm end soon?

Yes, _____. _____
end in a few hours.

2. Will Carol and Dave be in the office today?

No, _____. They're on vacation.

3. Will you return soon?

Yes, _____. _____
return in a little while.

4. Will Jane be in school tomorrow?

No, _____. She has a bad
cold.

5. Will you and Ray get out of work soon?

Yes, _____. _____
get out in half an hour.

B. Circle the correct answers.

1. I'm not going to fix that wire. I'm

afraid I | might | get a shock.
          | should |

2. What do you think?

| Might | I order the chicken or the fish?
| Should |

3. When I grow up I | might | be a
                      | should |

dentist, or I | might | be a doctor.
               | should |

4. It's going to rain. You | might | take
                              | should |

your umbrella.

C. Complete the conversations.

Ex. A. Are these Maria's gloves?

B. No. They aren't _____hers_____.

1. A. Is that your video camera?

B. No. It isn't _____.

2. A. Is that your son's computer?

B. No. It isn't _____.

3. A. Is that Mr. and Mrs. Baker's house?

B. No. It isn't _____.

4. A. Is this my recipe for meatballs?

B. No. It isn't _____.

D. Fill in the blanks.

Ex. Donald is _____neater than_____ Sam.
                        neat

1. Jane is _____ Sarah.
                 tall

2. Carl is _____ Jack.
                honest

3. Centerville is _____ Lakeville.
                       pretty

4. The pie is _____ the cake.
                   good

5. Julie is _____ John.
                 dependable

E. Complete the sentences.

Ex. William (rich) _____isn't as_____
_____rich as_____ Walter, but he's
much (happy) _____happier_____ .

1. Ann's printer (fast) _____
_____ Betty's printer, but it's much
(reliable) _____.

2. Danny's dog (friendly) _____
_____ Dorothy's dog, but it's much
(cute) _____.

3. Howard (intelligent) _____
_____ Mike, but he's much (interesting)
_____.

4. My apartment (fashionable) _____
_____ your
apartment, but it's much (big)
_____.

5. Tom's furniture (expensive) _____
_____ John's
furniture, but it's much (attractive)
_____.

F. Fill in the blanks.

Ex. Brian is _____the smartest_____ person
  _{smart}
I know.

1. Marvin is _____ person
  _{quiet}
I know.

2. Uncle Bert is _____
  _{hospitable}
person in our family.

3. We have _____
  _{large}
apartment in the building.

4. Mr. Peterson is _____
  _{patient}
teacher in our school.

5. Mel is _____ person
  _{lazy}
I know.

G. Listen and circle the correct answer.

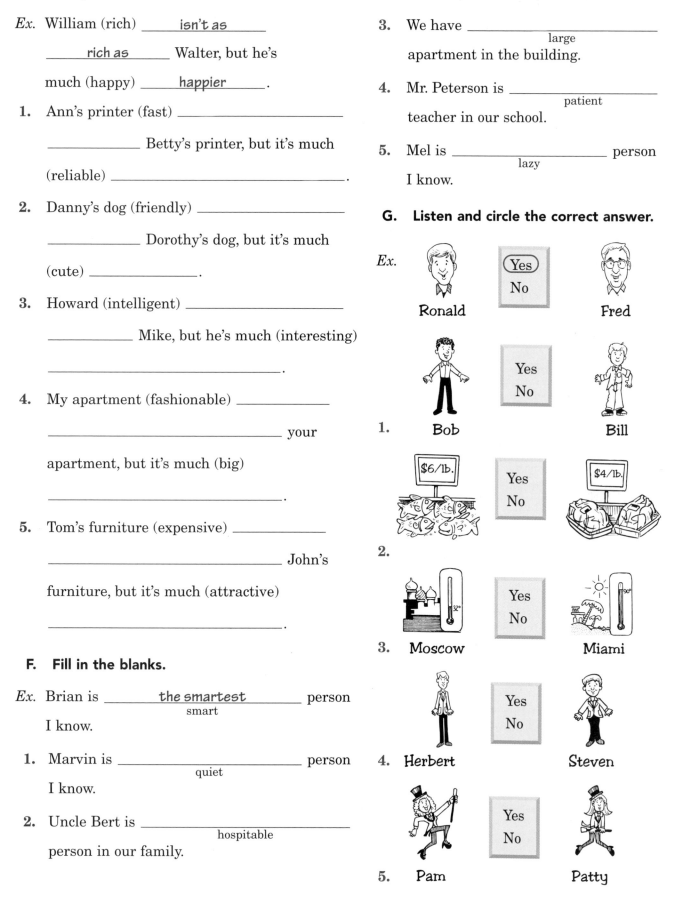

Ex. Ronald   (Yes) / No   Fred

1. Bob   Yes / No   Bill

2. $6/lb.   Yes / No $4/lb.

3. Moscow   Yes / No   Miami

4. Herbert   Yes / No   Steven

5. Pam   Yes / No   Patty

A HOW DO I GET THERE?

across from	on the right	walk up
between	on the left	walk down
next to		

7

SOUTH ST.

barber shop	library
clinic	toy store
shoe store	post office
bakery	book store
bank	drug store
high school	police station

1. A. Excuse me. Can you tell me how to get to the library from here?

   B. ___Walk up___ South Street and you'll see the library ___on the right___, ___across from___ the barber shop.

2. A. Excuse me. Can you tell me how to get to the clinic from here?

   B. _____ South Street and you'll see the clinic _____, _____ the shoe store.

3. A. Excuse me. Can you tell me how to get to the toy store from here?

   B. _____ South Street and you'll see the toy store _____, _____ the clinic.

4. A. Excuse me. Can you tell me how to get to the drug store from here?

   B. _____ South Street and you'll see the drug store _____, _____ the book store and the police station.

5. A. Excuse me. Can you tell me how to get to the high school from here?

   B. _____ South Street and you'll see the high school _____, _____ the bank and _____ the police station.

B WHICH WAY?

across from
between
next to
on the left
on the right

walk along
walk down
walk up

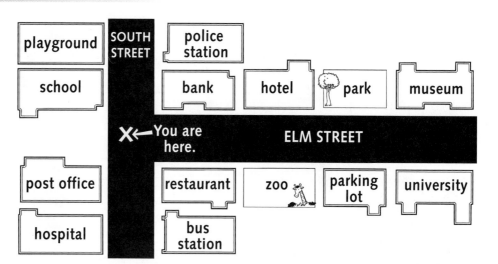

| playground | SOUTH STREET | police station |
| school | | bank | hotel | park | museum |

X ←You are here.   ELM STREET

| post office | | restaurant | zoo | parking lot | university |
| hospital | | bus station |

1. A. Excuse me. Could you please tell me how to get to the university from here?

   B. ____Walk along____ Elm Street and you'll see the university ____on the right____, ____across from____ the museum.

2. A. Excuse me. Could you please tell me how to get to the park from here?

   B. _____ Elm Street and you'll see the park

   _____, _____ the hotel.

3. A. Excuse me. Could you please tell me how to get to the police station from here?

   B. _____ South Street and you'll see the police station

   _____, _____ the playground.

4. A. Excuse me. Could you please tell me how to get to the bus station from here?

   B. _____ South Street and you'll see the bus station

   _____, _____ the restaurant.

5. A. Excuse me. Could you please tell me how to get to the zoo from here?

   B. _____ Elm Street and you'll see the zoo

   _____, _____ the restaurant and the parking lot.

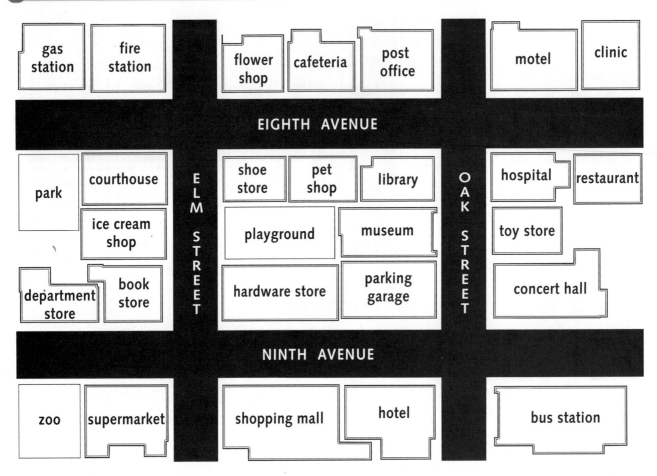

Mr. and Mrs. Lee are very busy today. They want to go several places with their children, but they don't know the city very well. They need your help.

1. They're at the shopping mall, and they want to take their children to the toy store to buy them a new toy. Tell them how to get there.

_____Walk along_____ Ninth Avenue to Oak Street and _____turn left_____. _____Walk up_____ Oak Street and you'll see the toy store _____on the right_____, _____across from_____ the museum.

2. They're at the toy store, and now they want to take their children to the pet shop to buy them a dog.

_____ Oak Street to Eighth Avenue and _____. _____ Eighth Avenue and you'll see the pet shop _____, _____ the shoe store and the library.

3. They're at the pet shop, and they want to take their children to the ice cream shop for some ice cream.

_____ Eighth Avenue to Elm Street and _____ . _____ Elm Street and you'll see the ice cream shop _____ , _____ the courthouse.

4. They're at the ice cream shop, and they want to take their children to the zoo.

_____ Elm Street to Ninth Avenue and _____ . _____ Ninth Avenue and you'll see the zoo _____ , _____ the department store.

5. They're at the zoo, and they're tired. They want to go to the park to rest.

....
....
....
....

6. They had a wonderful day, and now it's time to go home. Tell them how to get to the bus station.

....
....
....
....

D LISTENING

Look at the map on page 62. Listen and choose the correct answer.

1. a. She was hungry.
   b. She wanted to buy a bird.

2. a. He wanted to look at paintings.
   b. He wanted to listen to music.

3. a. They wanted to read some books.
   b. They wanted to buy some flowers.

4. a. She wanted to buy some toys for her son.
   b. She wanted to visit her sick friend.

5. a. He wanted to buy some groceries.
   b. He wanted to look at the animals.

6. a. She was sick.
   b. She was hungry.

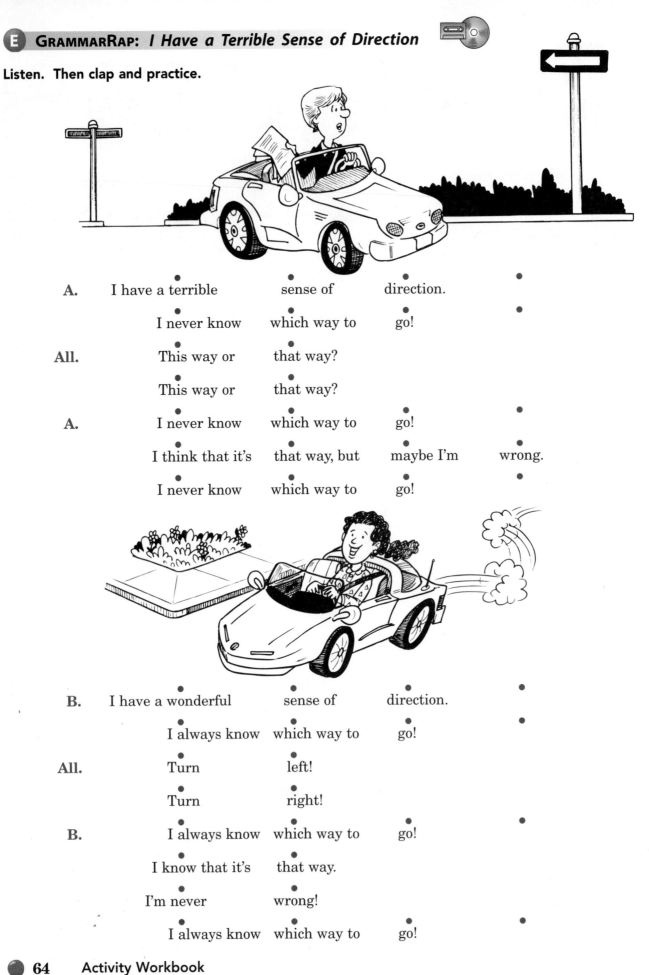

Listen. Then clap and practice.

A. I have a terrible sense of direction.
I never know which way to go!

All. This way or that way?
This way or that way?

A. I never know which way to go!
I think that it's that way, but maybe I'm wrong.
I never know which way to go!

B. I have a wonderful sense of direction.
I always know which way to go!

All. Turn left!
Turn right!

B. I always know which way to go!
I know that it's that way.
I'm never wrong!
I always know which way to go!

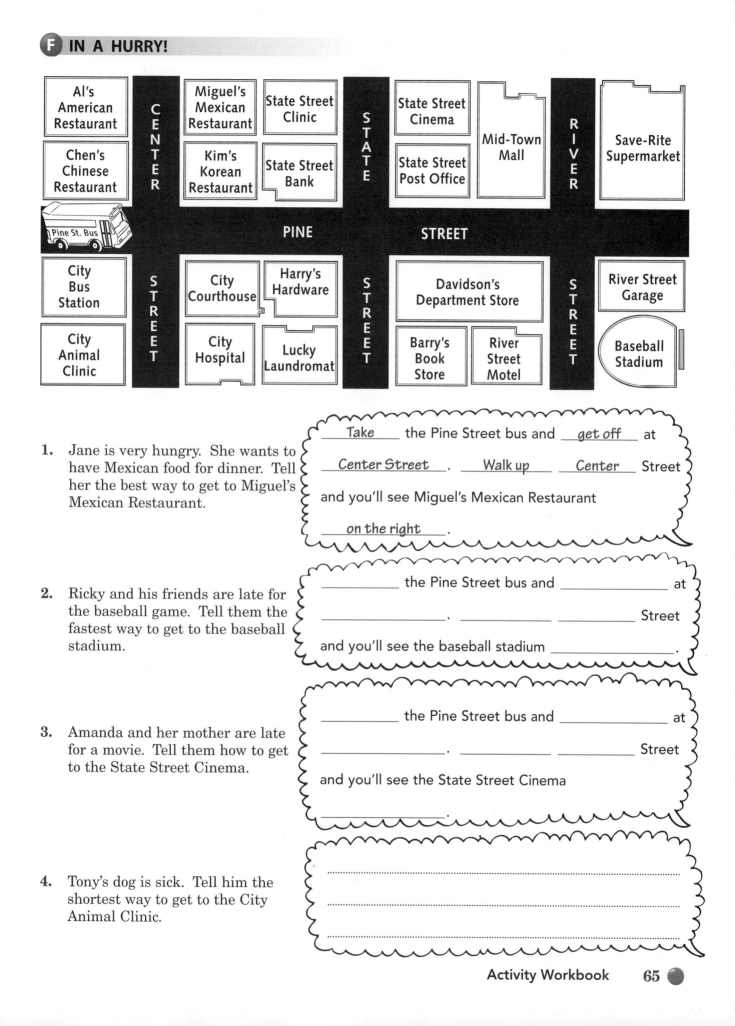

1. Jane is very hungry. She wants to have Mexican food for dinner. Tell her the best way to get to Miguel's Mexican Restaurant.

___Take___ the Pine Street bus and ___get off___ at ___Center Street___. ___Walk up___ ___Center___ Street and you'll see Miguel's Mexican Restaurant ___on the right___.

2. Ricky and his friends are late for the baseball game. Tell them the fastest way to get to the baseball stadium.

_____ the Pine Street bus and _____ at _____. _____ _____ Street and you'll see the baseball stadium _____.

3. Amanda and her mother are late for a movie. Tell them how to get to the State Street Cinema.

_____ the Pine Street bus and _____ at _____. _____ _____ Street and you'll see the State Street Cinema _____.

4. Tony's dog is sick. Tell him the shortest way to get to the City Animal Clinic.

Listen. Then clap and practice.

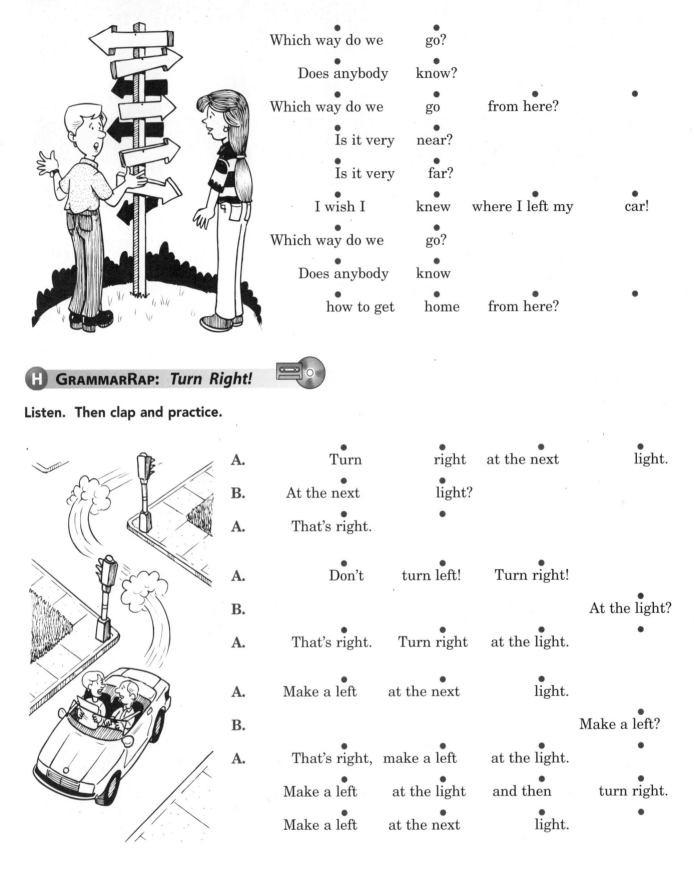

Which way do we go?

Does anybody know?

Which way do we go from here?

Is it very near?

Is it very far?

I wish I knew where I left my car!

Which way do we go?

Does anybody know

how to get home from here?

H GRAMMARRAP: *Turn Right!*

Listen. Then clap and practice.

A.   Turn   right   at the next   light.

B.   At the next   light?

A.   That's right.

A.   Don't   turn left!   Turn right!

B.   At the light?

A.   That's right.   Turn right   at the light.

A.   Make a left   at the next   light.

B.   Make a left?

A.   That's right,   make a left   at the light.

Make a left   at the light   and then   turn right.

Make a left   at the next   light.

I LISTENING: *Where Did They Go?*

DAY STREET

Day St. Bus				

<table>
<tr><td colspan="3">shopping mall</td><td rowspan="2" style="vertical-align:middle">F I R S T</td><td colspan="3">museum</td><td rowspan="2" style="vertical-align:middle">S E C O N D</td><td colspan="3">hospital</td><td rowspan="2" style="vertical-align:middle">T H I R D</td></tr>
<tr><td>bakery</td><td>bus station</td><td>hotel</td><td>ice cream shop</td><td>motel</td><td>clinic</td><td>high school</td><td>post office</td><td>park</td></tr>
</table>

BRIGHTON BOULEVARD

<table>
<tr><td>barber shop</td><td>book store</td><td>drug store</td><td rowspan="2" style="vertical-align:middle">S T R E E T</td><td>parking lot</td><td>toy store</td><td>gas station</td><td rowspan="2" style="vertical-align:middle">S T R E E T</td><td>police station</td><td>bank</td><td>pet shop</td><td rowspan="2" style="vertical-align:middle">S T R E E T</td></tr>
<tr><td>concert hall</td><td colspan="2">zoo</td><td>flower shop</td><td>library</td><td>church</td><td>shoe store</td><td>parking garage</td><td>fire station</td></tr>
</table>

BAY AVENUE

Bay Ave. Bus	

Listen and fill in the correct places.

1. He went to the _____ bank _____ .

2. She went to the _____ .

3. They went to the _____ .

4. She went to the _____ .

5. They went to the _____ .

6. He went to the _____ .

J WHAT'S THE WORD?

between	could	from	how	off	subway	turn	walk
certainly	excuse	get	left	please	take	up	

A. ____Excuse____ [1] me. _____ [2] you _____ [3]

tell me _____ [4] to _____ [5] to the train

station _____ [6] here?

B. _____ [7]. _____ [8] the

_____ [9] and get _____ [10] at Park Street.

Walk _____ [11] Park Street to Tenth Avenue

and _____ [12] right. _____ [13] along Tenth

Avenue and you'll see the train station on the

_____ [14], _____ [15] the post office

and the fire station.

A WHAT DO YOU THINK?

1. A. I think Barbara is a terrible dancer. What do you think?

   B. I agree. She dances _____terribly_____ .

2. A. Is Edward an accurate translator?

   B. He certainly is. He translates very _____.

3. A. I think Susan is a graceful swimmer.

   B. I agree. She swims very _____.

4. A. Is George a bad painter?

   B. Yes, he is. He paints very _____.

5. A. Is Rita a careful worker?

   B. Yes. She works very _____.

6. A. I think Fred is a dishonest card player.

   B. I agree. He plays cards very _____.

7. A. I think Roger is a careless skier.

   B. You're right. He skis very _____.

8. A. Your sister Jill is a very slow eater.

   B. I agree. She eats very _____.

9. A. Is Robert a _____ runner?

   B. Yes. He runs very fast.

10. A. I think Ron is a _____ skater.

    B. He certainly is. He skates very beautifully.

11. A. Is Margaret a _____ worker?

    B. Yes, she is. She works very hard.

12. A. I think Frank is a _____ baker.

    B. I agree. He bakes very well.

B ANSWER

CAREFUL
CAREFULLY

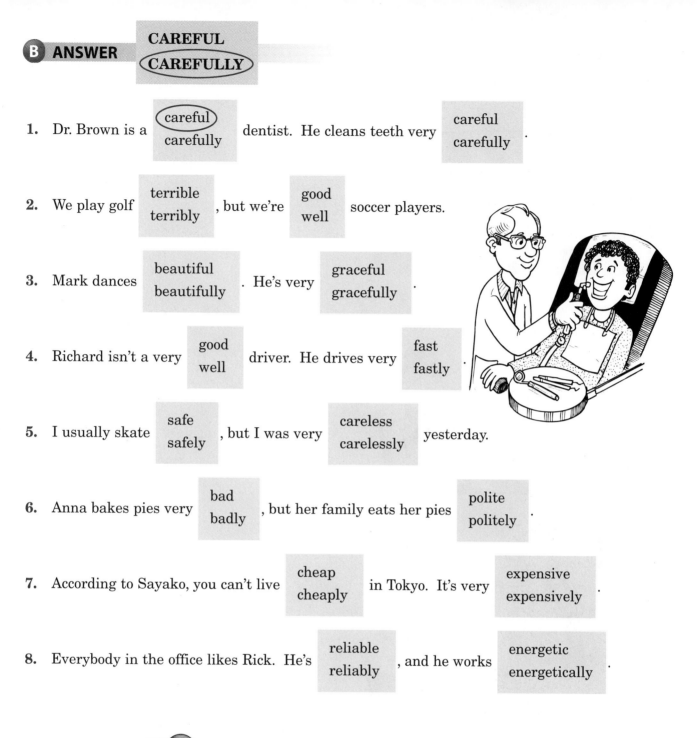

1. Dr. Brown is a (careful / carefully) dentist. He cleans teeth very (careful / carefully) .

2. We play golf (terrible / terribly) , but we're (good / well) soccer players.

3. Mark dances (beautiful / beautifully) . He's very (graceful / gracefully) .

4. Richard isn't a very (good / well) driver. He drives very (fast / fastly) .

5. I usually skate (safe / safely) , but I was very (careless / carelessly) yesterday.

6. Anna bakes pies very (bad / badly) , but her family eats her pies (polite / politely) .

7. According to Sayako, you can't live (cheap / cheaply) in Tokyo. It's very (expensive / expensively) .

8. Everybody in the office likes Rick. He's (reliable / reliably) , and he works (energetic / energetically) .

C LISTENING

Listen and circle the correct word to complete the sentence.

1. (slow) slowly
2. beautiful beautifully
3. dishonest dishonestly
4. sloppy sloppily

5. accurate accurately
6. rude rudely
7. safe safely
8. reliable reliably

9. soft softly
10. cheap cheaply
11. careful carefully
12. patient patiently

Listen. Then clap and practice.

A.   How am I   doing?

Am I driving   all right?

B.   You're driving very   carefully.

You're driving very   well.

A.   How am I   doing?

Am I singing   all right?

B.   You're singing very   beautifully.

You're singing very   well.

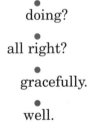

A.   How am I   doing?

Am I dancing   all right?

B.   You're dancing very   gracefully.

You're dancing very   well.

A.   How am I   doing?

Am I working   all right?

B.   You're working very   hard.

You're working very   well.

1. A. Am I jogging fast enough?
   B. You should try to jog

   _____ *faster* _____.

2. A. Harold isn't speaking loudly enough.
   B. I agree. He should speak

   _____.

3. A. Am I typing carefully enough?
   B. Actually, you should type

   _____.

4. A. Is he translating accurately enough?
   B. No, he isn't. He should translate

   _____.

5. A. Rob, I don't think you're doing your work quickly enough.
   B. I'm sorry. I'll try to do my work

   _____.

6. A. I know I'm not dancing gracefully enough.
   B. You're right. You should dance

   _____.

7. A. Am I cleaning the office well enough?
   B. Actually, you should clean it

   _____.

8. A. Is the new mechanic working hard enough?
   B. I think he should work

   _____.

9. A. Amanda, be careful! You aren't driving slowly enough!

   B. I'm sorry, Mr. Sanders. I'll try to drive _____.

RALPH SHOULD TRY HARDER!

Ralph has some problems. What should he do to make his life better?

1. Ralph always gets up very late.

   He should try to get up _____earlier_____.

2. He sometimes dresses very sloppily.

   He should try to dress _____.

3. He always eats breakfast very quickly.

   He should try to eat _____.

4. He sometimes speaks rudely on the bus.

   He should try to speak _____.

5. He usually works very slowly.

   He should try to work _____.

6. He sometimes types carelessly.

   He should try to type _____.

7. He plays his CD player very loudly every night.

   He should try to play it _____.

G **WHAT SHOULD *YOU* TRY TO DO BETTER?**

I should try to ....

I should try to ....

I should try to ....

I should try to ....

H GrammarSong: *Try a Little Harder*

Listen and circle the words to the song. Then listen again and sing along.

Let's say you're a driver, a (careful) / carefully [1] driver who

drives very careful / carefully [2] , as careful / carefully [3] drivers do.

Just try a little harder. You can find a way. Try to drive more careful / carefully [4] today.

Let's say you're a singer, a beautiful / beautifully [5] singer who

sings very beautiful / beautifully [6] , as beautiful / beautifully [7] singers do.

Just try a little harder. You can find a way. Try to sing more beautiful / beautifully [8] today.

Let's say you're a dancer, a graceful / gracefully [9] dancer who

dances very graceful / gracefully [10] , as graceful / gracefully [11] dancers do.

Try a little harder. You can find a way. Try to dance more graceful / gracefully [12] today.

Just try a little harder. That's what we always say. Sing a little strong / stronger [13] . Work a little

long / longer [14] . Do a little good / better [15] every day. Do a little good / better [16] every day.

I WHAT'S THE ANSWER?

1. If Helen _____ sick tomorrow, she'll go to work.
   a. isn't
   b. won't be

2. If the mechanic at Al's Garage fixes our car, _____ to the beach.
   a. we drive
   b. we'll drive

3. If _____ to your grandparents, they'll be very happy.
   a. you write
   b. you'll write

4. If Betty doesn't buy a VCR, _____ a CD player.
   a. she buys
   b. she'll buy

5. If you don't use enough butter, the cake _____ very good.
   a. isn't
   b. won't be

6. If _____ a course with Professor Boggs, I know it'll be boring.
   a. I take
   b. I'll take

7. If it _____ this Saturday, I think I'll go skiing.
   a. snows
   b. will snow

8. If you send me an e-mail, _____ right away.
   a. I answer
   b. I'll answer

9. If you _____ any more potatoes, I'll have rice with my chicken.
   a. don't have
   b. won't have

10. If the weather _____ good tomorrow, we'll play tennis.
    a. is
    b. will be

11. If I go on the roller coaster with you, I know _____ sick.
    a. I get
    b. I'll get

12. If you go there on your vacation, I'm sure _____ a good time.
    a. you have
    b. you won't have

J MATCHING

_d_ 1. If you stay on the beach all day,

____ 2. If you use fresh oranges,

____ 3. If you wear safety glasses,

____ 4. If you follow my directions to the zoo,

____ 5. If you don't eat breakfast,

____ 6. If you have a successful interview,

a. you won't get hurt.

b. you'll be hungry.

c. you won't get lost.

d. you'll get a sunburn.

e. you'll get the job.

f. the juice will be better.

K IF

1. If we _____arrive_____ early, _____we'll_____ visit your mother.

2. If _____ this afternoon, I'll wear my new raincoat.

3. If the weather _____ good, my husband and I _____ sailing.

4. If David _____ golf this weekend, _____ a wonderful time.

5. If you _____ a lot of noise, your neighbors _____ upset.

6. If your son _____ those wires, _____ a shock.

7. If _____ cold this Saturday, our family _____ skiing.

8. If Patty _____ too much candy, _____ a stomachache.

9. If I _____ too many exercises, _____ tired tonight.

10. If we _____ a girl, _____ her Patty.

11. If _____ a lot of traffic this morning, Nancy _____ probably be late for work.

12. If your parents _____ to Stanley's Restaurant on Monday, _____ _____ Italian food.

L SCRAMBLED SENTENCES

1. to   suit.   If   he   he'll   party,   goes   new   his   the   wear

    _____If he goes to the party_____ , _____he'll wear his new suit_____ .

2. late   she   work.   she'll   be   If   bus,   the   misses   for

    _____ , _____ .

3. better.   practice,   I   chess   play   I'll   If

    _____ , _____ .

4. buy   go   I   I'll   pie.   an   If   bakery,   the   apple   to

    _____ , _____ .

5. you   sorry.   If   finish   school,   be   you'll   don't

    _____ , _____ .

6. Sam   a   works   job.   in   good   If   he'll   hard   get   school,

    _____ , _____ .

M YOU DECIDE

Complete the sentences any way you wish.

1. If the weather is bad this weekend, ...

2. If I go to bed very late tonight, ...

3. If I don't eat dinner today, ...

4. If my computer breaks, ...

5. If I make a terrible mistake at school or at work, ...

6. If ...., they'll go to a special restaurant tonight.

7. If ...., his mother will be very happy.

8. If ...., his parents will be sad.

9. If ...., his boss will fire him.

10. If ...., my friends will be angry with me.

N GRAMMARRAP: *If You Leave at Six*

Listen. Then clap and practice.

If you leave at	six,
You'll be there at	eight.
If you don't leave	now,
You'll be very	late.
If you start work	now,
You'll be through at	seven.
If you wait 'till	noon,
You'll be busy 'till	eleven.
If you catch the	train,
You'll be home by	ten.
If you get there	late,
You'll miss dinner	again.

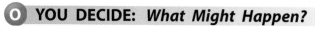

1. You shouldn't worry so much.

   If you worry too much, you might _____

2. Charlie shouldn't do his work so carelessly.

   If he does his work too carelessly, he might _____

3. Harriet shouldn't go to bed so late.

   If she goes to bed too late, she might _____

4. Your friends shouldn't use the Internet so much.

   If they use the Internet too much, they might _____

5. You shouldn't talk so much.

   If _____ , _____

6. Veronica shouldn't eat so much.

   If _____ , _____

7. Brian shouldn't buy so many expensive clothes.

   If _____ , _____

8. Your friends shouldn't play their music so loud.

   If _____ , _____

9. Raymond shouldn't speak so impolitely to his boss.

   If _____ , _____

10. You shouldn't speak so loudly.

    If _____ , _____

A. Please don't send me a lot of e-mail messages today!

B. Why not?

A. If you send me a lot of e-mail messages today, I'll have to read them tonight.

If ___I have to read___ [1] them tonight, _____I'll_____ [2] be tired tomorrow morning.

And if _____ [3] tired tomorrow morning, I'll fall asleep at work.

If _____ [4] at work, my boss _____ [5] be

understanding, and _____ [6] shout at me.

So please don't send me too many e-mail messages today!

A. Please don't play your CD player so loud!

B. Why not?

A. If you play your CD player too loud, the neighbors will be upset.

If _____ [7] upset, they'll tell the landlord.

And if _____ [8] the landlord, _____ [9] get angry.

So please don't play your CD player so loud!

A. Please don't buy Jimmy a scary video!

B. Why not?

A. If you buy him a scary video, _____ [10] be afraid when he

goes to sleep. If _____ [11] afraid when he goes to sleep,

_____ [12] have nightmares all night. If _____ [13]

nightmares all night, he _____ [14] get up on time. If

_____ [15] get up on time, _____ [16] late

for school. And if _____ [17] late for school, _____ [18]

miss a big test. So please don't buy Jimmy a scary video!

✓ CHECK-UP TEST: Chapters 7–8

A.   Complete the sentences.

Ex. She's a beautiful singer.

She sings very ___beautifully___ .

1. He's a terrible tennis player.

He plays tennis _____ .

2. She's a careful driver.

She drives very _____ .

3. They're bad cooks.

They cook very _____ .

4. I'm a hard worker.

I work very _____ .

B.   Circle the correct answers.

1. He isn't an honest / honestly player.

He plays dishonest / dishonestly .

2. The bus is quick / quickly , but it isn't

quiet / quietly .

3. Mario is a good / well soccer player,

but he doesn't run very good / well .

4. Alice usually drives safe / safely , but

last night she was careless / carelessly .

C.   Complete the sentences.

Ex. Timothy talks too quickly.
He should try to talk ___{slower / more slowly}___ .

1. Greta leaves work too early.

She should try to leave work

_____ .

2. Bobby speaks too impolitely at school.

He should try to speak _____

_____ .

3. Linda dances too awkwardly.

She should try to dance _____

_____ .

4. Frank talks too softly.

He should try to talk _____ .

D.   Complete the sentences.

Ex. If Jack ___does___ his homework, his

teacher ___will be___ happy.

1. If you _____ too many cookies,

_____ get a stomachache.

2. If the music _____ too loud,

the neighbors _____ angry.

3. If they _____ a boy,

_____ him Steven.

4. If _____ hungry tonight,
I'll eat a small dinner.

(continued)

E. Circle the correct answers.

1. If [we take / we'll take] a vacation this year, [we go / we'll go] to Hawaii.

2. If they [feel / will feel] energetic tonight, they [go / might go] dancing.

3. If you sing too loudly, you [get / might get] a sore throat.

4. If it [won't / doesn't] rain tomorrow, [I go / I'll go] sailing.

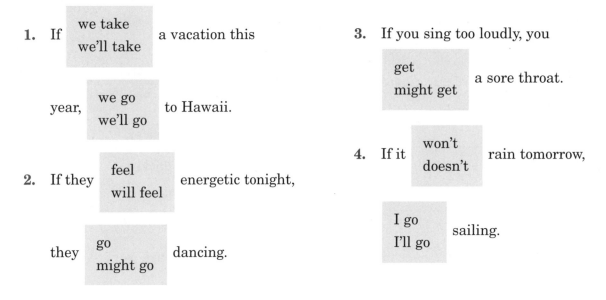

F. Listen and fill in the correct places.

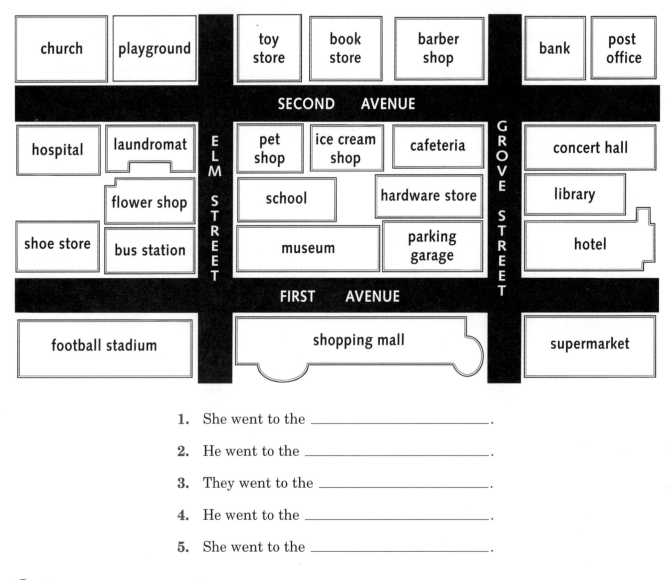

1. She went to the _____.

2. He went to the _____.

3. They went to the _____.

4. He went to the _____.

5. She went to the _____.

driving to the beach   playing basketball
fixing her fence   riding his motorcycle
jogging   skateboarding
painting their house   walking down Main Street

1. What was Paul doing when it started to rain?

        He was driving to the beach.

2. What was Diane doing when it started to rain?

3. What were Mr. and Mrs. Adams doing?

4. What were you and your friends doing?

5. What was Nick doing?

6. What was Natalie doing?

7. What were Tony and Mary doing?

8. What were you and Mike doing?

9. What were YOU doing?

....

B WHAT WERE THEY DOING?

1. My children (bake) _____were baking_____ a cake when I got home from work.

2. He (wear) _____ a helmet when he hit his head.

3. They (play) _____ tennis when it started to rain.

4. She (ride) _____ on a roller coaster when she got sick.

5. We (watch) _____ a movie when we fell asleep.

6. He (sleep) _____ at his desk when his boss fired him.

7. They (have) _____ an argument when the guests arrived.

8. I (chat) _____ online when the lights went out.

9. She (talk) _____ to her friend when the teacher asked her a question.

C GRAMMARRAP: *Standing Around*

Listen. Then clap and practice.

We were singing and dancing and standing around,
Laughing and talking and standing around.

Susan was singing.
Danny was dancing.
Stella and Stanley were standing around.

Lucy was laughing.
Tommy was talking.
Stuart and Steven were standing around.

We were singing and dancing and standing around,
Laughing and talking and standing around.

D THE WRONG DAY!

Alan and his wife were very embarrassed when they arrived at the Franklins' house yesterday. They thought the Franklins' party was on Friday. But the Franklins' party wasn't on Friday. It was on Saturday!

bake	clean	make	sweep	vacuum	wash

1. What was Mr. Franklin doing when they arrived?

___He was cleaning___ the dining room.

2. What was Mrs. Franklin doing when they arrived?

_____ the living room rug.

3. What was Tommy Franklin doing?

_____ the kitchen floor.

4. What was his sister Lucy doing?

_____ the windows.

5. What were Mrs. Franklin's parents doing?

_____ spaghetti.

6. What were Mr. Franklin's parents doing?

_____ cakes and cookies.

E LISTENING

Listen and choose the correct answer.

1. a. He was shaving.
   b. He was shopping.

2. a. She was skateboarding.
   b. She was skating.

3. a. They were sitting on the beach.
   b. They were swimming at the beach.

4. a. He was studying math.
   b. He was taking a bath.

5. a. We were reading.
   b. We were eating.

6. a. She was talking with her mother.
   b. She was walking with her brother.

7. a. He was taking a shower.
   b. He was planting flowers.

8. a. I was sleeping in the living room.
   b. I was sweeping the living room.

1. When I saw her, she was getting

   on
   off
   (into)

   a taxi on Main Street.

2. Al was walking

   out of
   off
   of

   the park when

   he fell.

3. I got

   from
   off
   up

   the bus and walked to

   the bank.

4. We went

   into
   out of
   at

   a restaurant because

   we were hungry.

5. Get

   at
   up
   on

   the subway at

   Sixth Avenue.

6. Ann was skating

   through
   along
   in

   Center Street.

7. I'm getting

   out of
   off
   up

   the car

   because I'm sick.

8. Susie got

   off
   to
   at

   the

   merry-go-round.

Listen and put the number under the correct picture.

___ ___ ___ ___

___ ___ _1_ ___

Listen. Then clap and practice.

A.   I called you   all day   today,

But you never   answered your   phone.

B.   That's strange! I was   here from   morning 'till   night.

I was home   all day   all alone.

A.   What were you   doing when I   called at   nine?

B.   I was probably   hanging my   clothes on the   line.

A.   What were you   doing when I   called at   one?

B.   I was probably   sitting   outside in the   sun.

A.   What were you   doing when I   called at   four?

B.   I was painting the   hallway and   fixing the   door.

A.   What were you   doing when I   called at   six?

B.   I was washing the   dog to get   rid of his   ticks.

A.   Well, I'm sorry I   missed you when I   tried to   phone.

B.   It's too bad. I was   here. I was   home   all alone.

I   NOBODY WANTS TO

| myself | yourself | himself | herself | ourselves | yourselves | themselves |

1. Nobody wants to go fishing with me.

   I'll have to go fishing by _____myself_____.

2. Nobody wants to drive to the beach with her.

   She'll have to drive to the beach by _____.

3. Nobody wants to go to the circus with us.

   We'll have to go to the circus by _____.

4. Nobody wants to go to the playground with you.

   You'll have to go to the playground by _____.

5. Nobody wants to eat lunch with them.

   They'll have to eat lunch by _____.

6. Nobody wants to watch the video with him.

   He'll have to watch the video by _____.

7. Nobody wants to play volleyball with you and your brother.

   You'll have to play volleyball by _____.

J   WHAT'S THE WORD?

1. My husband and I like to have a picnic by _____.
   a. ourselves
   b. ourself

2. Bobby likes to drink his milk by _____.
   a. hisself
   b. himself

3. My mother and father drove to the mountains by _____.
   a. themself
   b. themselves

4. My grandmother likes to take a walk in the park by _____.
   a. herself
   b. herselves

5. I like to do my homework by _____.
   a. myself
   b. yourself

6. You and your brother like to fix the car by _____.
   a. yourself
   b. yourselves

K WHAT HAPPENED?

bite	cook	drop	fall	have	lose	ride	shave	steal	walk
burn	cut	faint	get on	hurt	paint	roller-blade	ski	trip	watch

1. Jane ___tripped___ while ___she___ ___was walking___ down the stairs.

2. A dog _____ Johnny while _____ _____ his bicycle.

3. Sam _____ while _____ _____ a scary video.

4. Someone _____ our car while _____ _____ dinner at a restaurant.

5. Diane _____ her packages while _____ the bus.

6. I _____ myself while _____ _____.

7. Mr. and Mrs. Ling _____ themselves while _____ on the barbecue.

8. Brian _____ his wallet while _____.

9. We _____ ourselves while _____.

10. A can of paint _____ on them while _____ their house.

WHAT'S THE WORD?

1. We were walking
   - through
   - into
   - (up)
   the stairs.

2. They were driving
   - out of
   - over
   - down
   a bridge.

3. A heavy book fell
   - on
   - out of
   - along
   me.

4. They were walking
   - on
   - along
   - out of
   the bank.

5. She was working
   - into
   - at
   - over
   her office.

6. Let's go jogging
   - through
   - along
   - over
   the park!

7. Don't walk
   - under
   - over
   - in
   a ladder!

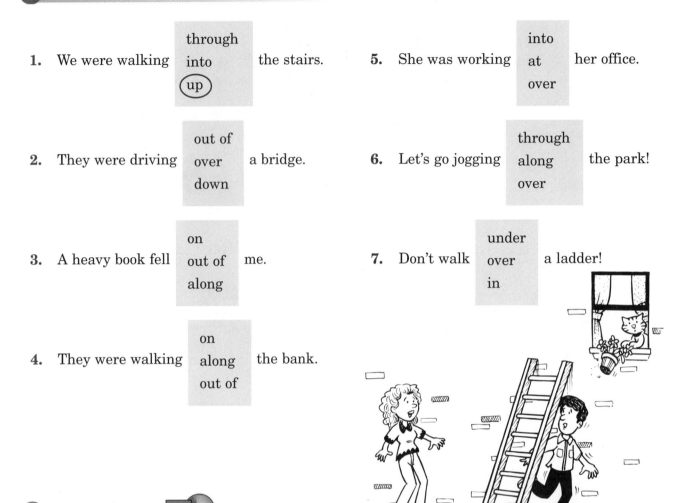

M **LISTENING**

Listen and choose the correct answer.

1. (a.) She lost her new boot.
   b. She lost her new suit.

2. a. He hurt himself while he was cooking.
   b. He burned himself while he was cooking.

3. a. While they were walking into the bank.
   b. While they were walking out of the park.

4. a. Someone stole our new fan.
   b. Someone stole our new van.

5. a. I dropped my new CD player.
   b. I dropped my new DVD player.

6. a. A dog bit him while he was working.
   b. A dog bit him while he was walking.

7. a. We were driving under a bridge.
   b. We were driving over a bridge.

8. a. She tripped and fell on the kitchen floor.
   b. She tripped and fell near the kitchen door.

9. a. While they were walking down the stairs.
   b. While they were walking up the stairs.

10. a. She was cooking on the barbecue.
    b. She was walking on Park Avenue.

11. a. I cut myself while I was chopping.
    b. I cut myself while I was shopping.

12. a. He waited at the bus stop.
    b. He fainted at the bus stop.

Listen. Then clap and practice.

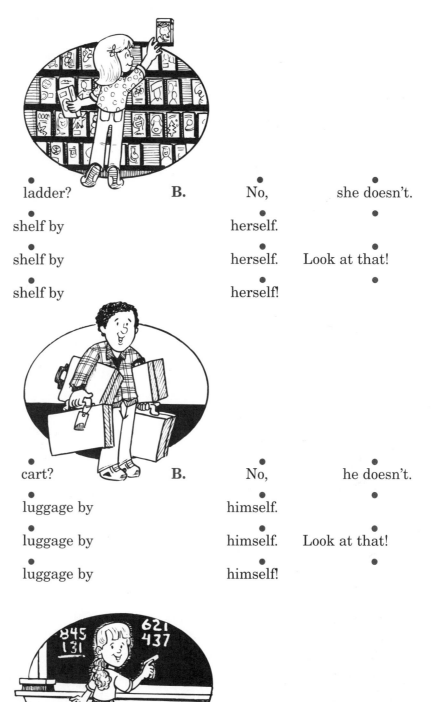

A. Does she need a ladder?

She can reach the top shelf by herself.

All. She can reach the top shelf by herself. Look at that!

She can reach the top shelf by herself!

B. No, she doesn't.

A. Does he need a cart?

He can carry all the luggage by himself.

All. He can carry all the luggage by himself. Look at that!

He can carry all the luggage by himself!

B. No, he doesn't.

A. Do you need a calculator?

I can add all these numbers by myself.

All. You can add all those numbers by yourself. Look at that!

You can add all those numbers by yourself!

B. No, I don't.

O LOUD AND CLEAR   he! him!

Fill in the words. Then read the sentences aloud.

e-mail	Greece	reading
niece	keypal	

1. My ___niece___ Louise is _____

   an _____ from her _____

   in _____.

cheese	asleep	fifteen	cookies
Steve		three	

3. _____ fell _____ at _____

   _____. He ate too many _____

   and too much _____.

beach	she's	Lee	Tahiti
CDs		sleeping	

5. Mr. and Mrs. _____ are on the _____

   in _____. He's _____, and

   _____ listening to _____.

himself	building	William	his
tripped		office	

2. _____ _____ and hurt

   _____ in front of _____

   _____ _____.

busy	children	Hill	sick
clinic		city	

4. Dr. _____ is very _____ at his

   _____. A lot of _____

   in the _____ are _____today.

sandwich	isn't	milk	little
spilled		sister	

6. My _____ _____ Jill _____

   very happy. She dropped her _____

   and _____ her _____.

could   can
couldn't   can't

10

1. Before I took lessons from Mrs. Rossini, I _____couldn't_____ play the violin very well.

   Now I _____can_____ play the violin beautifully.

2. I'm sorry you _____ go to the beach with us last weekend. Maybe you

   _____ go with us next weekend.

3. When I first arrived in this country, I was frustrated because I _____ speak

   English. Now I'm happy because I _____ speak English very well.

4. We _____ hear him because he spoke too softly.

5. We really want to fire Howard, but we _____. His father is president of the
   company.

6. My parents tell me that I was a very bright little girl. According to them, I_____

   read when I was two years old, and I _____ write when I was three years old.

7. We _____ move the refrigerator by ourselves because it was too heavy.

8. I _____ go to work yesterday because I was sick. But today I'm feeling much

   better. I'm sure I _____ go to work tomorrow.

9. Michael _____ go to lunch with his co-workers because he was too busy.

10. I _____ play basketball when I was in high school because I was too short. But

    I wasn't upset because I _____ play on the baseball team.

11. I'm disappointed. We _____ barbecue tonight. It's raining.

12. I _____ ask my boss for a raise. I was too nervous.

B GRAMMARRAP: *They Couldn't*

Listen. Then clap and practice.

A. She tried on the skirt, but she couldn't zip it up.

B. Was it too small?

A. Much too small.

A. She tried on the shoes, but she couldn't keep them on.

B. Were they too big?

A. Much too big.

A. He tried to talk, but he couldn't say a word.

B. Was he too nervous?

A. Much too nervous.

A. She sat at the table, but she couldn't eat a thing.

B. Was she too excited?

A. Much too excited.

A. He went to the lecture, but he couldn't stay awake.

B. Was he too tired?

A. Much too tired.

A. She took the course, but she couldn't pass the test.

B. Was it too hard?

A. Much too hard.

C YOU DECIDE: *Why Weren't They Able to?*

wasn't able to	weren't able to

1. Daniel _____ wasn't able to _____ lift the package

   because _____ it was too heavy _____ (*or*)

   _____ he was too tired _____ (*or*)

   _____ he was too weak. _____

2. Barbara _____ go to work yesterday because _____

   _____

3. My grandparents _____ finish their dinner because _____

   _____

4. Jim _____ buy the car he wanted because _____

   _____

5. I _____ get on the bus this morning because _____

   _____

6. The students in my class _____ solve the puzzle because _____

   _____

7. Maria _____ fall asleep last night because _____

   _____

8. My brother _____ wear my tuxedo to his wedding because _____

   _____

9. We _____ go sailing last weekend because _____

   _____

10. Robert _____ say "I love you" to his girlfriend because _____

    _____

D WHAT'S THE WORD?

{ could / was/were able to } { couldn't / wasn't/weren't able to } had to

1. The bus was very crowded this morning. I __{couldn't / wasn't able to}__ sit. I ___had to___ stand.

2. Carlos was very disappointed. He _____ take his daughter to the circus on

   Saturday because he _____ work overtime.

3. When I was young, I was very energetic. I _____ run five miles every day.

4. When Judy was ten years old, her family moved to a different city. She was sad because she

   _____ see her old friends very often.

5. When I was a little boy, I was upset because my older brothers _____ go

   to bed late, but I _____ . I _____ go to bed at 7:30
   every night.

6. We're sorry we _____ go to the tennis match with you yesterday. We

   _____ take our car to the mechanic.

7. When I was a teenager, I was very athletic. I _____ play baseball, and I

   _____ play football. But I was a terrible singer and dancer. I

   _____ sing, and I _____ dance.

8. My wife and I _____ go to our son's soccer game after school yesterday

   because we _____ meet with our lawyer.

9. Brian was upset because he wanted to have long hair, but he _____ . He

   _____ go to the barber every month because his parents liked very short hair.

E YOU DECIDE: *Why Didn't They Enjoy Themselves?*

myself ourselves yourself yourselves himself themselves herself	couldn't wasn't able to weren't able to

1. I didn't enjoy _____myself_____ at the beach yesterday. It was very windy, and I ___couldn't go swimming___ (or) ___wasn't able to go sailing___

2. Jim and his friends didn't enjoy _____ at the movie yesterday. It was very scary, and they _____

3. Nancy didn't enjoy _____ at the museum. It was very crowded, and she _____

4. Edward didn't enjoy _____ at the restaurant last night. The food was very spicy, and he _____

5. I didn't enjoy _____ at the circus last Friday. It was very noisy, and I _____

6. We didn't enjoy _____ on our vacation last winter. We got sick, and we _____

F WHAT'S THE WORD?

1. Walter was pleased. He didn't have to call the plumber. He ____ fix the sink himself.
   a. couldn't
   b. was able to *(circled)*

2. I ____ get to work on time this morning because the bus was late.
   a. was able to
   b. couldn't

3. I missed the company picnic yesterday because I ____ go to the eye doctor.
   a. had to
   b. wasn't able to

4. We ____ finish our dinner because we were too full.
   a. could
   b. weren't able to

5. I forgot my briefcase, and I ____ to go back home and get it.
   a. wasn't able to
   b. had

6. We ____ fall asleep last night. Our neighbors played their music very loudly.
   a. couldn't
   b. were able to

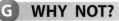

I've	she's	they've	
he's	we've	you've	got to

Tomorrow afternoon David is moving to a new apartment next door. He asked a lot of people to help him, but unfortunately, everybody is busy tomorrow afternoon, and nobody will be able to help him. They all have things they've got to do.

1. His friend Bob won't be able to help him.

    _____He's got to_____ take his daughter to the doctor.

2. His friend Sandra won't be able to help him.

    _____ drive her brother to the train station.

3. I'm sorry. I won't be able to help you.

    _____ take care of my neighbor's little boy.

4. Tom and I won't be able to help you, either.

    _____ stay home and wait for the plumber.

5. David's brother won't be able to help him.

    _____ study for an important English test.

6. David's cousins won't be able to help him.

    _____ go to baseball practice.

7. We're really sorry, David.

    Unfortunately, _____ move to your new apartment by yourself.

MY FRIEND LISA

> will / won't be able to

My friend Lisa is an active, energetic person.

1. She goes jogging every morning.
2. She rides her bicycle to school every day.
3. She plays tennis on the school team.
4. She swims every afternoon.
5. She does exercises every evening.

She's also very talented and capable.

6. She plays the violin.
7. She bakes delicious cakes and cookies.
8. She makes her own clothes.
9. She fixes her computer when it's broken.

Last week on Friday the 13th Lisa went skating, and unfortunately, she broke her leg. The doctor says she'll have to rest her leg all month. Lisa is very upset.

1. _____She won't be able to go jogging every morning._____

2. _____

3. _____

4. _____

5. _____

Fortunately, there are many things that Lisa WILL be able to do.

6. _____She'll be able to play the violin._____

7. _____

8. _____

9. _____

THEY'LL BE ABLE TO

> couldn't   will be able to

1. My daughter ____couldn't____ go to her ballet lesson today, but I'm sure ____she'll be able to____ go next week.

2. We _____ assemble our new lamp yesterday. I hope _____ assemble it today.

3. Bill _____ go to football practice today. He thinks _____ go to football practice tomorrow.

4. I _____ fall asleep last night. I hope _____ fall asleep tonight.

Activity Workbook   **97**

J   THEY WON'T BE ABLE TO

won't be able to	have/has got to

1. I'm sorry. I _____won't be able to_____ cook dinner tonight.

   _____I've got to_____ work overtime.

2. I'm terribly sorry. My daughter _____ baby-sit

   this afternoon. _____ practice the violin.

3. My children _____ eat ice cream at the party.

   Their doctor told them_____ eat fruit for dessert.

4. I'm really upset. My father _____ lend us money

   because _____ buy a new van.

5. Unfortunately, my husband and I _____ play golf

   with you today. _____ take our dog to the vet.

K   LISTENING

Listen to each story, and then choose the correct answers to the questions you hear.

William's New Apartment

1. a. He was able to open his living room windows.
   b.) He couldn't open his living room windows.

2. a. The lights in his apartment went out.
   b. His apartment is too bright.

3. a. He won't be able to cook dinner.
   b. He'll be able to watch his favorite programs on TV.

Mr. and Mrs. Clark's New Computer

4. a. They could assemble their computer easily.
   b. They weren't able to assemble their computer easily.

5. a. Their computer crashed.
   b. They used their new computer.

6. a. They'll be able to call their grandchildren.
   b. They won't be able to send any e-mail to their grandchildren.

L GRAMMARRAP: *Were You Able to?*

Listen. Then clap and practice.

A. Were you able to leave early last night?

B. No. I had to work until seven.

A. Were you able to get to the office on time?

B. No. I couldn't get there 'till eleven.

A. Were you able to take the six o'clock bus?

B. No. I had to wait until eight.

A. Were you able to get to the meeting on time?

B. No. I had to walk in late.

M GRAMMARRAP: *They Won't Be Able to*

Listen. Then clap and practice.

A. Will you be able to join us for dinner?

B. No, I won't. I've got to work late.

A. Will he be able to meet us tomorrow?

B. No, he won't. He's got to see Kate.

A. Will she be able to come to the meeting?

B. No, she won't. She's got to call Jack.

A. Will they be able to go on the sightseeing trip?

B. No, they won't. They've got to unpack.

Listen and fill in the words to the song. Then listen again and sing along.

day	do	go	no	play	to	today

My friend Jim called the other ____day____ [1].

He said, "Would you like to see a play _____ [2]?"

I didn't really want to _____ [3], so this is how I told him _____ [4].

I'm afraid I won't be able _____ [5]. I have a lot of things to _____ [6].

I've got to wash my clothes and clean my house today.

But thank you for the invitation. I want to express my appreciation.

I'm sure that we'll be able to see a _____ [7] another _____ [8].

My friend Bob called the other _____ [9].

He said, "Would you like to roller-skate _____ [10]?"

I didn't really want to _____ [11], so this is how I told him _____ [12].

I'm afraid I won't be able _____ [13]. I have a lot of things to _____ [14].

I've got to paint my house and bathe my cat today.

But thank you for the invitation. I want to express my appreciation.

I'm sure that we'll be able to roller-skate another day.

I'm sure that we'll be able to.

I'm sure that we'll be able to.

✔ CHECK-UP TEST: Chapters 9–10

A. Complete the sentences.

Ex. She (wash) __was washing__ her hair when the lights went out.

1. We (play) _____ basketball when it started to rain.

2. I (drive) _____ my car when I crashed into a tree.

3. They (jog) _____ in the park when the snow began.

4. Marvin cut himself while he (shave) _____ this morning.

5. A thief stole our car while we (read) _____ in the library.

6. She fell on the sidewalk while she (ride) _____ her bicycle.

7. I got paint all over myself while I (sit) _____ on a bench in the park.

B. Fill in the blanks.

Ex. I enjoyed __myself__ at the museum.

1. We didn't enjoy _____ at the concert.

2. Richard burned _____ while he was cooking on the barbecue.

3. Did you and your husband enjoy _____ at the party?

4. Did you fix the VCR by _____, or did your wife help you?

5. Mr. and Mrs. Lopez cut _____ while they were fixing their fence.

6. Nobody went skating with Kate. She had to go skating by _____.

C. Circle the correct answers.

1. When I saw Jill, she was getting [off / of / in] a bus.

2. I usually get [at / up / on] the subway at First Street.

3. When the teacher walked [out of / off / of] the room, everybody started to talk.

4. We run [through / off / on] the park every day.

5. They were walking [from / into / at] the bank when I saw them.

6. The mail carrier [could / couldn't / can't] deliver our mail yesterday because our dog bit him.

7. I'm sorry you [couldn't / were able to / won't be able to] go to the baseball game with us tomorrow.

(continued)

8. When I was a teenager, I wanted to go out with my friends every night, but I

could		could	
couldn't	because I	couldn't	study.
had to		had to	

D. Fill in the blanks.

1. Bill _____ able to go to the beach yesterday because it was raining.

2. I'm glad you _____ able to help me with my science project next weekend.

3. Sally and Jane _____ able to walk home from the party because it was too dark.

4. I couldn't pay my rent last month, but

I'm sure _____ able to pay it next month.

5. I'm sorry I _____ able to arrive on time yesterday afternoon.

I _____ fix a flat tire.

6. If you want to put your hair in a ponytail,

_____ got to have long hair.

7. My daughter _____ able to go to school next week because

_____ got to have an operation.

E. Listen to the story, and then choose the correct answers to the questions you hear.

Poor Janet!

1. a. She could dance in the school play.
   b. She wasn't able to dance in the school play.

2. a. She practiced every day.
   b. She didn't practice.

3. a. She fell down and cut herself.
   b. She fell down and hurt herself.

4. a. She'll be able to dance in the play.
   b. She can't dance in the play this year.

A MATCHING

You're going for a checkup tomorrow. What will happen?

_d_	1. The nurse will lead you	**a.**	a chest X-ray.
____	2. You'll stand	**b.**	your heart with a stethoscope.
____	3. The nurse will measure	**c.**	about your health.
____	4. A lab technician will do	**d.**	into an examination room.
____	5. An X-ray technician will take	**e.**	your height and weight.
____	6. The doctor will listen to	**f.**	a cardiogram.
____	7. The doctor will do	**g.**	on a scale.
____	8. The doctor will talk to you	**h.**	some blood tests.

B HOW WAS YOUR MEDICAL CHECKUP?

1. I had a complete _____.
   a. health
   b. examination ⓑ

2. First, the nurse led me into _____.
   a. a test
   b. an examination room

3. I _____ on a scale.
   a. stood
   b. examined

4. The nurse measured my _____.
   a. heart
   b. height

5. Then she _____ my blood pressure.
   a. took
   b. did

6. The lab technician did some _____.
   a. blood tests
   b. blood pressure

7. The doctor _____ my hand.
   a. look
   b. shook

8. He _____ my throat.
   a. listened
   b. examined

9. He did a _____.
   a. cardiogram
   b. stethoscope

10. He talked with me about my _____.
    a. healthy
    b. health

less	fewer	more

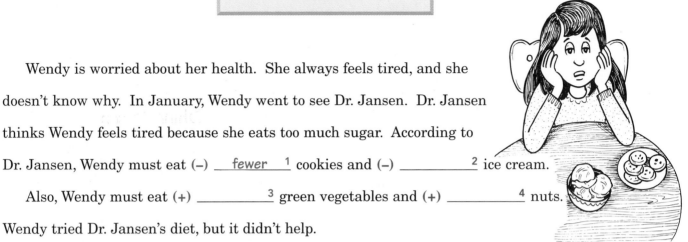

Wendy is worried about her health. She always feels tired, and she doesn't know why. In January, Wendy went to see Dr. Jansen. Dr. Jansen thinks Wendy feels tired because she eats too much sugar. According to Dr. Jansen, Wendy must eat (–) __fewer__ [1] cookies and (–) _____ [2] ice cream.

Also, Wendy must eat (+) _____ [3] green vegetables and (+) _____ [4] nuts. Wendy tried Dr. Jansen's diet, but it didn't help.

In March, Wendy went to see Dr. Martin. Dr. Martin thinks Wendy feels tired because she's too thin. According to Dr. Martin, Wendy must eat (–) _____ [5] vegetables and (–) _____ [6] lean meat. Also, Wendy must eat (+) _____ [7] candy and (+) _____ [8] potatoes. Wendy tried Dr. Martin's diet, but it didn't help.

In April, Wendy went to see Dr. Appleton. Dr. Appleton thinks Wendy feels tired because she eats too much spicy food. According to Dr. Appleton, Wendy must eat (–) _____ [9] pepper and (–) _____ [10] onions. Also, Wendy must drink (+) _____ [11] skim milk and (+) _____ [12] water. Wendy tried Dr. Appleton's diet, but it didn't help.

In May, Wendy went to see Dr. Mayfield. Dr. Mayfield thinks Wendy feels tired because she eats too much salt. According to Dr. Mayfield, Wendy must eat (–) _____ [13] french fries and (–) _____ [14] salt. Also, Wendy must eat (+) _____ [15] yogurt and (+) _____ [16] fish. Wendy tried Dr. Mayfield's diet, but it didn't help.

Now Wendy needs YOUR help. What do you think?

Wendy must eat/drink (–) _____

_____

Also, she must eat/drink (+) _____

_____

Listen. Then clap and practice.

Candy,   cookies,   ice cream, cake!

Candy,   cookies,   ice cream, cake!

Eat less   candy!

Fewer   cookies!

Eat less   ice cream!

Eat less   cake!

Candy,   cookies,   ice cream, cake!

Candy,   cookies,   ice cream, cake!

Carrots,   beans,   grapefruit, greens!

Carrots,   beans,   grapefruit, greens!

Eat more   carrots!

Eat more   beans!

Eat more   grapefruit!

Eat more   greens!

Carrots,   beans,   grapefruit, greens!

Carrots,   beans,   grapefruit, greens!

must		answer	dress	repair	type

1. Here at the Greenly Company, you
   ____must dress____ neatly, and
   you ____must type____ accurately.

2. Remember, you _____ the
   telephone politely, and you _____
   _____ the cars carefully.

must		arrive	file	sort	work

3. Here at the Tip Top Company, every
   employee _____ on time
   and _____ hard.

4. It's very important. You _____
   the mail carefully, and you _____
   _____ accurately.

must		cook	dance	sing	speak

5. Remember, Ginger, you _____
   gracefully, and you _____
   beautifully.

6. Here at Joe's Diner, you _____
   the food quickly, and you _____
   _____ to the customers politely.

F WHAT'S THE WORD?

mustn't	don't have to	doesn't have to

1. You _____mustn't_____ arrive late for work.

2. Helen's doctor is concerned. He says she _____ eat too much candy.

3. According to my doctor, I _____ stop jogging, but I _____ jog so often.

4. Tomorrow is a holiday. The store is closed. The employees _____ work.

5. It's early. You _____ leave right now. But remember, you _____ leave too late.

6. My landlord is upset. He says I _____ play music after midnight.

7. Charlie is lucky. He _____ call the plumber because he was able to fix the sink by himself.

G THE BUTLER SCHOOL

must	mustn't	don't have to

At the Butler School you _____must_____ [1] get to school on time

every morning. If you're late, your parents _____ [2] write a note.

If you're sick, your parents _____ [3] call the school.

You can bring your lunch if you want to, but you

_____ [4] because we have a very nice cafeteria.

The boys _____ [5] always wear jackets, but if they don't want to wear ties, they

_____ [6]. The girls _____ [7] wear dresses or skirts. Some girls want to wear

pants to school, but at the Butler School they _____ [8]. Everyone _____ [9]

have a notebook for every subject, and you _____ [10] forget to take your notebooks to

class. You can talk to your friends while you're working, but you _____ [11] talk too

loudly. You _____ [12] speak politely to your teacher, but you _____ [13] agree

with your teacher all the time. If you have a different opinion, your teacher will be happy to

listen. Finally, you _____ [14] always do your homework.

H WRITE ABOUT YOUR SCHOOL

At our school, you must _____

You mustn't _____

You don't have to _____

I YOU DECIDE: *What Did They Say?*

must	mustn't

1. My parents told me _____

_____ because I have a big test tomorrow.

2. Sally talked to her English teacher, and he told her _____

_____ because she makes too many mistakes.

3. Robert talked to his girlfriend and she told him _____

_____ because he works too much.

4. Grandpa talked to his doctor and she told him _____

_____ because he's a little too heavy.

5. We talked to our landlord and he told us _____

_____ because the neighbors are upset.

6. I talked to my grandmother and she told me _____

_____ because life is short.

Listen and choose the correct answer.

1. a. You should watch TV more often.
   b. (circled) You must stop watching TV so often.

2. a. You must lose some weight.
   b. You should start eating rich desserts.

3. a. I should stop eating spicy foods.
   b. I must start eating spicy foods.

4. a. You must stop relaxing.
   b. You must take life a little easier.

5. a. You must start listening to loud music.
   b. You should stop listening to loud music.

6. a. I must stop jogging.
   b. I should jog more often.

K **GRAMMARRAP:** *You Mustn't Eat Cookies*

Listen. Then clap and practice.

A.	You mustn't eat	cookies.
B.	You mustn't eat	cake.
C.	You mustn't eat	butter.
D.	You mustn't eat	steak.
A.	You must eat	fruit.
B.	You must eat	potatoes.
C.	You must eat	fish.
D.	You must eat	tomatoes.

L **GRAMMARRAP:** *You Must...*

Listen. Then clap and practice.

A.	You must clean your	room.
B.	But I cleaned it on	Sunday!
A.	You must do the	laundry.
B.	But I did it last	Monday!
A.	You must fix the	fence.
B.	But I fixed it in	June!
A.	You must do your	homework!
B.	I'll finish it	soon!

h!

Fill in the words. Then read the sentences aloud.

hotel	Hawaii	happy	here
	Hi	Honolulu	

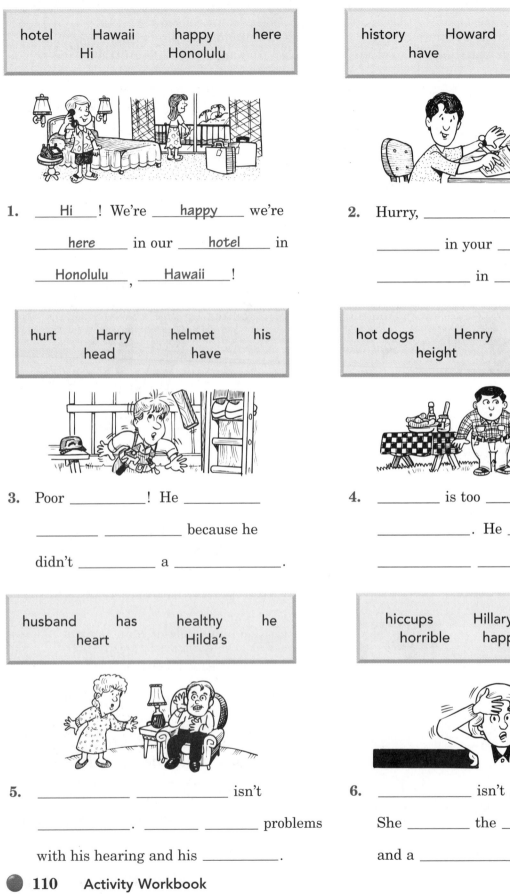

1. ___Hi___! We're ___happy___ we're

___here___ in our ___hotel___ in

___Honolulu___, ___Hawaii___!

history	Howard	half	hand
	have	homework	

2. Hurry, _____! You _____ to

_____ in your _____

_____ in _____ an hour.

hurt	Harry	helmet	his
	head	have	

3. Poor _____! He _____

_____ _____ because he

didn't _____ a _____.

hot dogs	Henry	has	heavy
	height	having	

4. _____ is too _____ for his

_____. He _____ to stop

_____ _____.

husband	has	healthy	he
	heart	Hilda's	

5. _____ _____ isn't

_____. _____ _____ problems

with his hearing and his _____.

hiccups	Hillary	headache	
horrible	happy	has	

6. _____ isn't _____.

She _____ the _____

and a _____ _____.

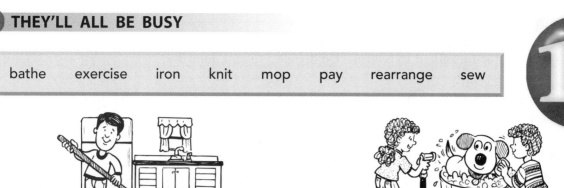

| bathe | exercise | iron | knit | mop | pay | rearrange | sew |

1. Will Michael be busy this morning?

   ___Yes, he will___ . ___He'll be mopping___
   his floors.

2. Will your children be busy this afternoon?

   _____ . _____
   the dog.

3. Will you and George be busy today?

   _____ . _____
   at the health club.

4. Will Mr. and Mrs. Benson be busy today?

   _____ . _____
   bills.

5. Will Kate be busy tomorrow afternoon?

   _____ . _____
   a sweater.

6. Will you be busy this afternoon?

   _____ . _____
   clothes.

7. Will Fred be busy this Saturday?

   _____ . _____
   shirts.

8. Will you and your wife be busy tomorrow?

   _____ . _____
   furniture.

Arthur was upset after he talked to Gloria. He decided to call Jennifer.

Hi, Jennifer. This is Arthur. Can I come over this afternoon?

No, Arthur. I'm afraid I won't be home this afternoon.

I'll be _____ .

I see. Can I come over TOMORROW afternoon?

No, Arthur. I'm afraid I won't be home tomorrow afternoon.

I'll be _____ .

Can I come over and visit this WEEKEND?

No, Arthur. I'll be _____ .

Well, can I come over and visit next Monday?

No, Arthur. I'll be _____ .

How about some time next AUTUMN?

No, Arthur. I'm getting married next autumn.

Oh, no! Not again!!

Listen. Then clap and practice.

A. What do you   think you'll be   doing next   spring?

B. I'll probably be   doing the   same old   thing.

A. What do you   think he'll be   doing this   fall?

B. I'm sure he'll be   working   downtown at the   mall.

A. When do you   think they'll be   leaving for   Spain?

B. I think they'll be   taking the   four o'clock   plane.

A. When do you   think you'll be   hearing from   Anne?

B. I'm sure she'll be   calling as   soon as she   can.

A. When do you   think we'll be   hearing from   Jack?

B. I'm sure he'll be   phoning as   soon as he's   back.

A. What do you   think she'll be   doing at   two?

B. I think she'll be   taking the   kids to the   zoo.

A. Where do you   think they'll be   living next   year?

B. As far as we   know, they'll be   living right   here.

bake	clean his apartment	exercise	study	wash her car
bathe their dog	do their laundry	practice the violin	take a bath	watch TV

1. A. Why don't you call Jane this Saturday?
    B. I don't want to disturb her. I'm sure

    _____she'll be practicing the violin_____.

    She always _____practices the violin_____
    on Saturday.

2. A. Why don't you call Carlos after dinner?
    B. I don't want to disturb him. I'm sure

    _____.

    He always _____
    after dinner.

3. A. Why don't you call Peggy and Bob
        tonight?
    B. I don't want to disturb them. I'm sure

    _____.

    They always _____
    on Monday night.

4. A. Why don't you call Nancy
        this afternoon?
    B. I don't want to disturb her. I'm sure

    _____.

    She usually _____
    in the afternoon.

5. A. Why don't you call your cousin Henry
        this morning?
    B. I don't want to disturb him. I'm sure

    _____.

    He always _____
    on Sunday morning.

6. A. Why don't you call Tom and Carol
        this evening?
    B. I don't want to disturb them. I'm sure

    _____.

    They always _____
    in the evening.

7. A. Why don't you call Elizabeth this this afternoon?
   B. I don't want to disturb her. I'm sure

   _____.

   She usually _____
   on Sunday afternoon.

8. A. Why don't you call your aunt and uncle this morning?
   B. I don't want to disturb them. I'm sure

   _____.

   They always _____
   on Saturday morning.

9. A. Why don't you call your friend George tonight?
   B. I don't want to disturb him. I'm sure

   _____.

   He always _____
   before he goes to bed.

10. A. Why don't you call Betty and Ben tonight?
    B. I don't want to disturb them. I'm sure

    _____.

    They always _____
    on Tuesday night.

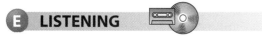 **E LISTENING**

Listen and choose the correct answer.

1. a. buying dresses
    b. ironing dresses

2. a. working downtown
    b. walking downtown

3. a. sitting on the front porch
    b. knitting on the front porch

4. a. watching sports
    b. washing shorts

5. a. feeding the baby
    b. reading to the baby

6. a. taking a bus
    b. taking a bath

7. a. making pancakes
    b. baking cakes

8. a. doing her homework
    b. doing yoga

9. a. skiing
    b. sleeping

10. a. skateboarding
    b. skating

11. a. washing the dog
    b. walking the dog

12. a. singing about you
    b. thinking about you

WHAT'S THE WORD?

called	isn't	message	right	take	that
hello	may	okay	speak	tell	this

A. _____Hello_____ ¹.

B. Hello. _____ ² is Brian. _____ ³ I please

_____ ⁴ to Cathy?

A. I'm sorry. Cathy _____ ⁵ here _____ ⁶ now.

Can I _____ ⁷ a _____ ⁸ ?

B. Yes. Please _____ ⁹ Cathy _____ ¹⁰

Brian _____ ¹¹.

A. _____ ¹².

B. Thank you.

G **WHAT'S THE RESPONSE?**

Choose the correct response.

1. May I please speak to Ronald?
   a. Thank you.
   b. Yes. Hold on a moment.

2. When can you come over?
   a. At three this afternoon.
   b. Don't worry.

3. I don't want to disturb you.
   a. Yes, I will.
   b. Don't worry. You won't disturb me.

4. We won't be able to come over and visit you tomorrow night.
   a. Oh. Why not?
   b. When?

5. I can come over tonight. Is that okay?
   a. I'll be glad.
   b. Sure. I'll see you then.

6. Sorry. I'll be eating dinner at seven.
   a. I don't want to disturb you.
   b. I'll disturb you.

7. Hello.
   a. Okay.
   b. Hello. This is Mrs. Miller.

8. Hi, Barbara. What's up?
   a. Fine.
   b. I'm having a test tomorrow.

9. I'm afraid I won't be home at three.
   a. Okay. I'll see you at three.
   b. Oh. How about six?

10. I'm having some problems with the homework for tomorrow.
    a. I'll be glad to help.
    b. I'm glad.

11. Will you be home this Wednesday afternoon?
    a. Yes. I'll be shopping.
    b. Yes. I'll be ironing.

12. How about nine o'clock?
    a. Fine. I'll see you then.
    b. Yes, it will.

at	for	in	until

1. A. How much longer will you be practicing the piano?

   B. ____I'll be practicing____ the piano

      __for__ another half hour.

2. A. How long will Grandpa be reading the newspaper?

   B. _____ the newspaper

      _____ he falls asleep.

3. A. How late will Jane be working at the office this evening?

   B. _____ at the office

      _____ ten o'clock.

4. A. Excuse me. When will we be arriving in San Francisco?

   B. _____ in San Francisco

      _____ six thirty.

5. A. When will you be having your yearly checkup?

   B. _____ my yearly

      checkup_____ a few weeks.

6. A. How late will Maria be studying English?

   B. _____ English

      _____ 8:30.

7. A. How long will your Uncle Willy be staying with us?

   B. _____ with us

      _____ next month.

8. A. How much longer will you be cooking on the barbecue?

   B. _____ on the barbecue

      _____ another ten minutes.

1. How much longer ___will you be talking on the telephone___ ?

I'll be talking on the telephone for another half hour.

2. A. How late _____ ?

   B. They'll be arriving at midnight.

3. A. How long _____ ?

   B. She'll be working on his car all morning.

4. A. When _____ ?

   B. He'll be leaving in a little while.

5. A. How far _____ ?

   B. We'll be driving until we get to Miami.

6. A. How long _____ ?

   B. I'll be mopping the floors all morning.

7. A. How soon _____ ?

   B. She'll be feeding the dog when she gets home.

8. A. How much longer _____ ?

   B. They'll be living away from home until they finish college.

9. A. How late _____ ?

   B. He'll be playing loud music until 2 A.M.

10. How much longer _____ ?

We'll be riding on the roller-coaster for another five minutes.

Listen. Then clap and practice.

A.   How much   longer will you be   talking on the   phone?

B.   I'll be talking for a   few more   minutes.

A.   For a few more   minutes?

B.   That's what I   said.

      I'll be talking for a   few more   minutes.

A.   How much   longer will he be   working   at the mall?

B.   He'll be working for a   few more   hours.

A.   For a few more   hours?

B.   That's what he   said.

      He'll be working for a   few more   hours.

A.   How much   longer will she be staying in   Rome?

B.   She'll be staying for a   few more   days.

A.   For a few more   days?

B.   That's what she   said.

      She'll be staying for a   few more   days.

13

me	him	her	us	you	them
my	his	her	our	your	their
myself	himself	herself	ourselves	yourself	themselves
				yourselves	

1. ___His___ family didn't help ___him___. He painted the fence by ___himself___.

2. _____ parents didn't help _____. They made breakfast by _____.

3. _____ mother usually helps _____ put her hair in a ponytail. But today she did it by _____.

4. Do you need any help? I'll help _____. _____ don't have to rake the leaves by _____.

5. Nobody is helping _____. He's washing the dishes by _____.

6. I planted these flowers by _____. Nobody helped _____.

7. _____ teacher can't help _____. We've got to do our homework by _____.

8. You don't have to go on the roller coaster by _____. I'll go with _____.

B THE LOST ROLLERBLADES

mine	his	hers	ours	yours	theirs

A. I just found these rollerblades. Are they ___yours___ ¹?

B. No. They aren't _____ ². But they might be Jim's. He always forgets things.

A. No. I don't think they're _____ ³. His rollerblades are green, and these are black.

B. Do you think they might be Ms. Johnson's?

A. Our English teacher's?! No. They can't be _____ ⁴. She doesn't have rollerblades.

B. How about Carol and Ted? Do you think these rollerblades might

be _____ ⁵?

A. No, I don't think so. They never go rollerblading. I have an idea. Let's put the rollerblades in the school office.

B. Okay. And if nobody asks for them soon, I guess they'll be _____ ⁶.

C SCRAMBLED SENTENCES

Unscramble the sentences.

1. his   he   by   fix   himself?   Did   car

   _____Did he fix his car by himself?_____

2. book   Is   yours?   address   this

   _____

3. cats   feed   by   She   can   the   herself.

   _____

4. you   number?   Did   her   him   telephone   give

   _____

5. Bob,   I   new   When   him   you   tell   call   his   sunglasses.   have

   _____

6. lost   because   to   cell   your   I   mine.   need   use   phone   I

   _____

Choose the correct word.

1. I like to eat the _____ stew.
   a. chef's
   b. chefs'

2. I love my _____ birthday presents!
   a. grandmother's
   b. grandmothers'

3. Where's the _____ food?
   a. cat's
   b. cats'

4. Do you listen to your _____ CDs?
   a. sons'
   b. son's

5. These are probably a _____ headphones.
   a. student's
   b. students'

6. Is this your _____ ring?
   a. girlfriends'
   b. girlfriend's

7. My _____ new painting is very ugly.
   a. cousin's
   b. cousins'

8. My _____ dog usually barks all night.
   a. neighbor's
   b. neighbors'

E **LISTENING**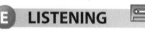

Listen to each conversation, and then choose the correct answers to the questions you hear.

CONVERSATION 1

1. a. On the floor.
   b. On the desk.
   c. On the chair.

2. a. No, it isn't his.
   b. It might be his.
   c. Yes, it's his.

3. a. Last Tuesday.
   b. Last Monday.
   c. Last Thursday.

CONVERSATION 2

4. a. Black.
   b. Brown.
   c. Blue.

5. a. Her watch.
   b. Her umbrella.
   c. Her wallet.

6. a. Yes, it's hers.
   b. No, it isn't hers.
   c. It might be hers.

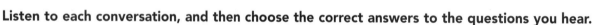

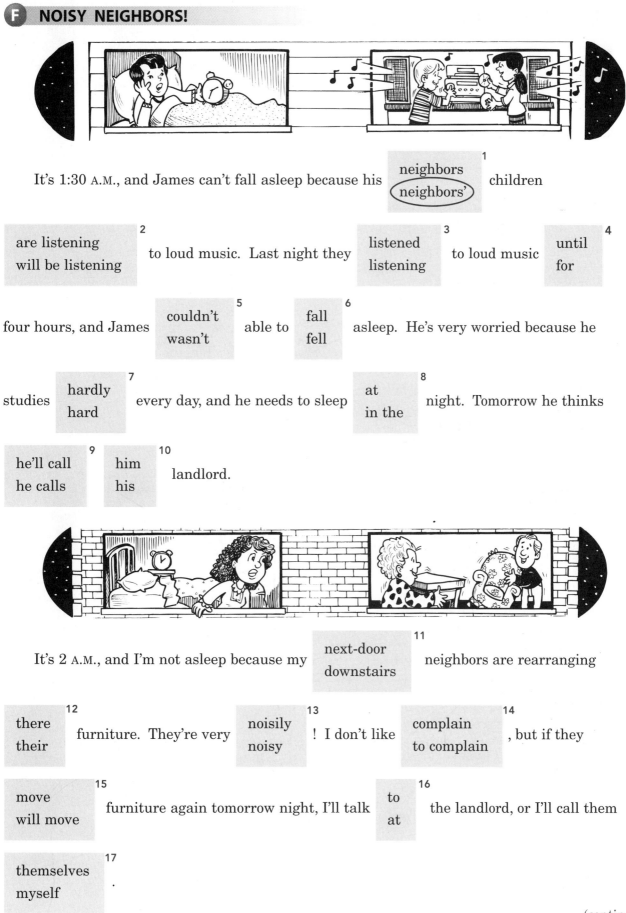

It's 1:30 A.M., and James can't fall asleep because his [neighbors / **neighbors'**]¹ children

[are listening / will be listening]² to loud music. Last night they [listened / listening]³ to loud music [until / for]⁴

four hours, and James [couldn't / wasn't]⁵ able to [fall / fell]⁶ asleep. He's very worried because he

studies [hardly / hard]⁷ every day, and he needs to sleep [at / in the]⁸ night. Tomorrow he thinks

[he'll call / he calls]⁹ [him / his]¹⁰ landlord.

It's 2 A.M., and I'm not asleep because my [next-door / downstairs]¹¹ neighbors are rearranging

[there / their]¹² furniture. They're very [noisily / noisy]¹³ ! I don't like [complain / to complain]¹⁴ , but if they

[move / will move]¹⁵ furniture again tomorrow night, I'll talk [to / at]¹⁶ the landlord, or I'll call them

[themselves / myself]¹⁷ .

(continued)

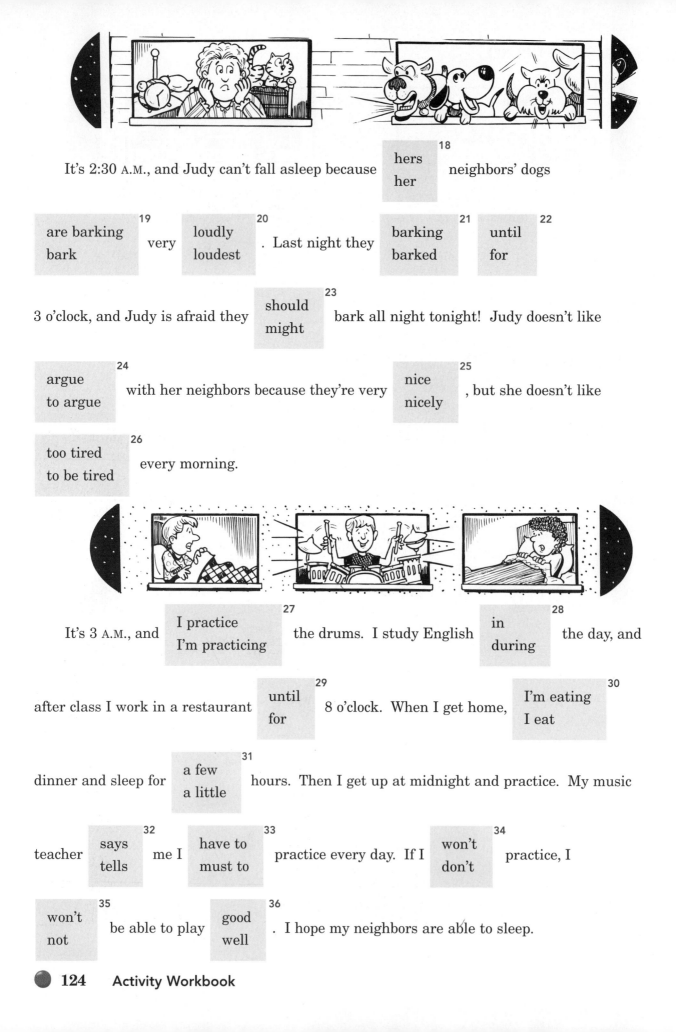

It's 2:30 A.M., and Judy can't fall asleep because [hers / her] [18] neighbors' dogs

[are barking / bark] [19] very [loudly / loudest] [20]. Last night they [barking / barked] [21] [until / for] [22]

3 o'clock, and Judy is afraid they [should / might] [23] bark all night tonight! Judy doesn't like

[argue / to argue] [24] with her neighbors because they're very [nice / nicely] [25], but she doesn't like

[too tired / to be tired] [26] every morning.

It's 3 A.M., and [I practice / I'm practicing] [27] the drums. I study English [in / during] [28] the day, and

after class I work in a restaurant [until / for] [29] 8 o'clock. When I get home, [I'm eating / I eat] [30]

dinner and sleep for [a few / a little] [31] hours. Then I get up at midnight and practice. My music

teacher [says / tells] [32] me I [have to / must to] [33] practice every day. If I [won't / don't] [34] practice, I

[won't / not] [35] be able to play [good / well] [36]. I hope my neighbors are able to sleep.

1. A. I don't like Stuart. He never says [anyone / (anything)] nice.

   B. To tell the truth, [nobody / anybody] likes Stuart. He never

   says [anything / something] nice about [nobody / anybody] !

2. A. I can't fix my video camera. Is there [anyone / anything] you can do to help?

   B. No. I'm afraid [nobody / somebody] here can help you.

   You'll have to fix it by [himself / yourself] .

3. A. Look! [Anybody / Somebody] ate all the cake!

   B. That's terrible! [Anybody / Nobody] will be able to

   have it for dessert tonight!

4. A. There's [anyone / someone] on the phone for you.

   B. Who is it?

   A. I don't have [any / some] idea.

(continued)

5. A. I can't hook up my new printer. Does [anybody / nobody] here know how to do it?

B. You should ask the supervisor. She knows [anyone / someone] who can do it.

6. A. How was the party last night?

B. It was terrible! I didn't know [anyone / somebody] there,

and [anybody / nobody] talked to me.

7. A. What's that noise? I think [anybody / somebody] is in the basement!

B. I don't hear [nothing / anything]. Don't worry. [Nobody / Anybody]

is in the basement.

A. Are you sure? I definitely hear [anything / something].

B. Don't worry. [Nobody / Anybody] is there.

H **LISTENING:** *The Prom*

Listen and choose the correct response.

1. a. No, I wasn't.
   (b.) I didn't enjoy myself very much.

2. a. It wasn't very comfortable.
   b. She was very talkative.

3. a. It was too crowded.
   b. It was too soft.

4. a. Until 10:30.
   b. In a few hours.

5. a. I missed the bus.
   b. I wasn't having a good time.

6. a. I'm sure it is.
   b. We'll just have to wait and see.

A. Hello. May I please speak to Maggie Winters?

B. ....

A. There's something wrong with my dishwasher, and I need a repairperson who can come over and fix it.

B. ....

A. No. There isn't any water on the kitchen floor, but the dishwasher won't turn on.

B. ....

A. I don't know. It worked yesterday, but it isn't working today.

B. ....

A. I live at 234 School Street in Westville.

B. ....

A. Drive down Center Street and turn right. My house is the last one on the left.

B. ....

A. I'm sorry. I'm afraid I won't be home at 9:00 tomorrow morning. Can you come at any other time?

B. ....

A. Can you come a little earlier?

B. ....

A. That's fine. I'll see you then. Good-bye.

B. Good-bye.

Listen. Then clap and practice.

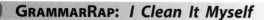

A.   Who cleans your   house?

B.   I clean it   myself.

A. Does your wife   help you?

B.   She helps me if I   ask her.

A.   Who does your   laundry?

B.   I do it   myself.

A. Does your husband   help you?

B.   He helps me if I   ask him.

A.   Who washes the   dishes?

B.   He washes them himself.

A. Does his daughter   help him?

B.   She helps him if he   asks her.

A.   Who makes   breakfast?

B.   She makes it   herself.

A. Does her father   help her?

B.   He helps her if she   asks him.

A.   Who does your   shopping?

B.   We do it   ourselves.

A. Do your children   help you?

B.   They help us if we   ask them.

A.   Who does their   homework?

B.   They do it   themselves.

A. Does their mother   help them?

B.   She helps them if they ask her.

K YOU DECIDE: *Why Can't They Go to the Baseball Game?*

A. Would you like to go to a baseball game with me on Saturday?

B. ....

A. That's too bad. Do you think your sister might be able to go?

B. ....

A. Oh, I forgot. She's busy every Saturday. How about your cousins? They like baseball.

B. ....

A. Oh. I hope they enjoy themselves. Do you think your father might want to go?

B. ....

A. That's too bad. Nobody told me. How did it happen?

B. ....

A. Well, I hope he's better soon. You know, I guess I'll go to work on Saturday.

B. ....

A. Really? Our boss likes baseball?!

B. ....

A. Okay. I'll call him and see if he wants to go with me. Good-bye.

B. ....

L LISTENING

Listen and choose the person you should call.

1. a. a plumber
   b. a mechanic
   c. a doctor

2. a. a lab technician
   b. an electrician
   c. a plumber

3. a. a doctor
   b. a locksmith
   c. a dentist

4. a. a mechanic
   b. a plumber
   c. the landlord

5. a. an electrician
   b. a plumber
   c. a painter

6. a. a mechanic
   b. the police
   c. a repairperson

7. a. a chef
   b. an electrician
   c. a plumber

8. a. a teacher
   b. a repairperson
   c. a mechanic

Circle the correct word.

1. **Too** / **(Two)** cats are **(too)** / **two** many cats for me!

2. Last **weak** / **week** I was too **weak** / **week** to get out of bed.

3. **Their** / **They're** going to go for **their** / **they're** annual physical examination.

4. You're **right** / **write** . I should **right** / **write** my term paper this weekend.

5. **Wear** / **Where** are my glasses? I need to **wear** / **where** them.

6. We have an **our** / **hour** to do **our** / **hour** exercises.

7. Do you **no** / **know** a good dentist? **No,** / **Know,** I don't.

8. You should **by** / **buy** a camera and take pictures of your children **by** / **buy** yourself.

9. There's a big **hole** / **whole** in my slice of **hole** / **whole** wheat bread!

10. **You're** / **Your** late. **You're** / **Your** guests arrived twenty minutes ago.

11. Yesterday they cooked **ate** / **eight** cakes for a party, and the guests **ate** / **eight** all the cakes.

Listen. Then clap and practice.

Does anybody   here speak   Spanish?

Does anybody   here speak   French?

Does anybody   here have a   hammer?

Does anyone   here have a   wrench?

Somebody   here speaks   Spanish.

Somebody   here speaks   French.

Somebody   here has a   hammer.

Someone   here has a   wrench.

Does anybody   here have   change for a   dollar?

Does anyone   here have   a dime?

Does anybody   here have a   map of the   city?

Does anyone   here have the   time?

Nobody   here has   change for a   dollar.

Nobody   here has   a dime.

Nobody   here has a   map of the   city.

Nobody   here has the   time.

A. Complete the sentences.

Ex. Will you be home this evening?
Yes, I will. (knit)

_____ I'll be knitting _____.

1. Will your parents be busy today?
Yes, they will. (pay)

_____ bills.

2. Will you be leaving home soon?
Yes, I will. (go)

_____ to college.

3. Will your brother be home at 5:00?
Yes, he will. (read)

_____ his e-mail.

4. Will Karen be at the office tonight?
Yes, she will. (work)

_____ until 9:00.

5. Will you and your girlfriend be busy
this Saturday?
Yes, we will. (get married)

_____ .

B. Complete the sentences.

Ex. When _____ will you be visiting us _____?
We'll be visiting you next January.

1. How late _____

_____ ?
I'll be practicing the piano until 8:00.

2. How much longer _____

_____ ?
He'll be ironing for a few more
minutes.

3. How soon _____

_____ ?
She'll be leaving in a little while.

4. How far _____

_____ ?
They'll be driving until they get to Denver.

5. How long _____

_____ ?
We'll be chatting online for a few hours.

C. Circle the correct answers.

1. My doctor says I must eat [less / fewer] ice cream,

[less / fewer] french fries, and [less / fewer] fatty meat.

2. I [mustn't / don't have to] solve this math problem

tonight, but I want to.

3. Jim [mustn't / doesn't have to] eat too [much / many]

spicy food because he has stomach problems.

4. If you want to get a job in this office, you must
speak English and Spanish, but you

[mustn't / don't have to] type very fast.

5. My son will be performing in the school

play [for / until] a week.

6. She'll be staying in Chicago [for / until] Friday.

7. They finished  [at / in] 8:00.

8. I'll be arriving [at / in] noon.

9. I need [anyone / someone] who can fix my camcorder. I don't know [anything / something] about camcorders.

10. If you look in the phone book, I'm sure you'll find [anybody / somebody] who can fix your VCR.

11. [Anyone / Someone] borrowed my mop, and now I can't clean the floors.

12. This is his car. It isn't [my / mine].

13. I don't think this is [their / theirs] cell phone, but it might be [her / hers].

14. We gave [her / his] our headphones.

15. This camera isn't [ours / our].

D. Listen and choose the correct answers to complete the sentences.

1. a. a complete physical examination.
   b. an examination room.

2. a. your blood.
   b. your height and your weight.

3. a. blood pressure.
   b. stethoscope.

4. a. a pulse.
   b. an X-ray.

5. a. eyes, ears, nose, and throat.
   b. checkup.

APPENDIX

Listening Scripts

Page 2 Exercise B

Listen and choose the correct response.

1. What do your friends like to do on the weekend?
2. What does your sister like to do on the weekend?
3. What does your brother like to do on the weekend?
4. What do you and your friends like to do on the weekend?
5. What does your son like to do on the weekend?
6. What do you like to do on the weekend?
7. What does your next-door neighbor like to do on the weekend?
8. What does your cousin Sue like to do on the weekend?

Page 10 Exercise N

Listen and write the ordinal number you hear.

Many people live and work in this large apartment building in New York City.

1. There's a barber shop on the second floor.
2. The Wong family lives on the twelfth floor.
3. The Acme Internet Company is on the thirtieth floor.
4. Bob Richards lives on the thirteenth floor.
5. There's a bank on the third floor.
6. There's a dentist's office on the ninth floor.
7. There's a flower shop on the first floor.
8. The Martinez family lives on the nineteenth floor.
9. Louise Lane works on the seventeenth floor.
10. There's a computer store on the fourth floor.
11. There's an expensive French restaurant on the forty-eighth floor.
12. My apartment is on the fifth floor.
13. The Park family lives on the thirty-fourth floor.
14. Dr. Jacobson has an office on the twenty-sixth floor.
15. The Walker family lives on the sixty-second floor.
16. There's a health club on the eighteenth floor.

Page 13 Exercise C

Listen and choose the correct response.

1. Where's the tea?
2. Where are the oranges?
3. Where's the fish?
4. Where are the cookies?
5. Where's the cake?
6. Where's the rice?
7. Where are the pears?
8. Where's the cheese?

Page 15 Exercise F

Listen and put a check under the correct picture.

1. Let's have some pizza!
2. Where are the eggs?
3. Let's make some fresh orange juice!
4. Let's bake a pie!
5. Where are the potatoes?
6. Let's have a sandwich for lunch!

Page 19 Exercise L

Listen and put a check under the correct picture.

1. A. Would you care for some more?
   B. Yes, please. But not too much.
2. A. Do you like them?
   B. Yes, but my doctor says that too many are bad for my health.
3. A. These are wonderful!
   B. I'm glad you like them. I bought them this morning.
4. A. How much did you eat?
   B. I ate too much!
5. A. I bought it this morning, and it's very good. Would you like a little?
   B. Yes, please.
6. A. I really don't like them.
   B. But they're good for you!
7. A. How do you like them?
   B. They're wonderful.
8. A. Would you care for some more?
   B. Yes, please. But not too much.
9. A. Hmm. This is delicious. Would you care for some more?
   B. Yes, please. But just a little.
10. A. This is delicious!
    B. I'm glad you like it. I made it this morning.

Page 22 Exercise C

Listen to the conversations. Put a check under the foods you hear.

1. A. Do we need anything from the supermarket?
   B. Yes. We need a pound of apples, a bunch of bananas, and a head of lettuce.
2. A. What do we need at the supermarket?
   B. We need a pound of cheese, a box of rice, and a bottle of soda.
3. A. Do we need anything from the supermarket?
   B. Yes. We need a loaf of bread, a pound of onions, and a dozen oranges.
4. A. What do we need at the supermarket?
   B. We need a pound of potatoes, a pint of ice cream, and a jar of mustard.

Page 24 Exercise F

Listen and circle the price you hear.

1. A box of cereal costs a dollar ninety-nine.
2. Two cans cost five dollars.
3. Three jars cost four dollars and seventy-nine cents.
4. It costs twenty-five cents.
5. A bottle costs two forty-seven.
6. Two boxes cost six dollars and sixty cents.
7. Three thirteen?! That's a lot of money!
8. A pound costs a dollar fifty.
9. Two dollars and ten cents?! That's cheap!

Page 27 Exercise M

Listen and choose the correct word to complete the sentence.

1. Add a little . . .
2. Chop up a few . . .
3. Cut up a few . . .
4. Pour in a little . . .
5. Slice a few . . .
6. Mix in a little . . .

Page 29 Exercise E

Listen and circle the correct word.

Ex. I want some lemons.
1. I'd like some ice cream.
2. I need some tomatoes.
3. I'm looking for lettuce.
4. May I have some meatballs?
5. I want some whole wheat bread.

Page 32 Exercise D

Listen and circle the words you hear.

1. I want to have the chocolate ice cream.
2. They won't fax the letter this morning.
3. I want to recommend the fish today.
4. Peter and William won't go home this morning.
5. She won't eat meat.
6. They want to get married soon.
7. He won't buy a car this year.
8. We want to use our computer now.

Page 37 Exercise K

Listen and choose the correct answer.

1. I'm afraid I might get sick!
2. I'm afraid I might fall asleep!
3. I'm afraid I might step on your feet!
4. I'm afraid I might break my leg!
5. I'm afraid I might catch a cold!
6. I'm afraid I might drown.
7. I'm afraid I might get seasick!
8. I'm afraid I might get a sunburn!
9. I'm afraid I might have a terrible time!
10. I'm afraid I might look terrible!

Page 42 Exercise F

Listen and choose the correct words to complete the sentences.

1. A. Yesterday was cool.
   B. I know. But today is . . .
2. A. Ronald is tall.
   B. You're right. But his son Jim is . . .
3. A. This briefcase is very attractive.
   B. Really? I think THAT briefcase is . . .
4. A. Nancy is very nice.
   B. Do you know her sister Sally? She's . . .
5. A. Tom is very fast.
   B. You're right. But his brother John is . . .
6. A. Michael is a very friendly person.
   B. I know. But his wife is . . .
7. A. Your roommate is very interesting.
   B. You're right. But I think YOUR roommate is . . .
8. A. The supermarket on Center Street was very busy today.
   B. Yes, I know. But the supermarket on Main Street was . . .

Page 44 Exercise I

Listen and circle the correct answer.

1. Yesterday was hotter than today.
2. The tomatoes are more expensive than the potatoes.
3. Aunt Betty is younger than cousin Jane.
4. Bob is shorter and heavier than Bill.
5. Barry's chair is more comfortable than Larry's chair.
6. The science test was more difficult than the history test.
7. Irene's office is bigger than Eileen's office.
8. Ronald is more capable than Donald.

Page 56 Exercise F

Listen and circle the words you hear.

1. My new chair is much more comfortable than my old chair.
2. Is that the worst city in the country?
3. I want a more energetic president.
4. Don't you have a cheaper one?
5. What was the most important day in your life?
6. Roger is the sloppiest teenager I know.
7. This is the best perfume we have.
8. Sally isn't as lazy as Richard is.
9. You know, I think your dog is meaner than mine.
10. Howard is the most honest person I know.

Page 59 Exercise G

Listen and circle the correct answer.

Ex. Ronald is younger than Fred.
1. Bob is neater than Bill.
2. The chicken is more expensive than the fish.
3. Moscow is warmer than Miami.
4. Herbert is taller than Steven.
5. Patty is more talented than Pam.

Page 63 Exercise D

Look at the map on page 62. Listen and choose the correct answer.

1. Linda was at the hotel on Ninth Avenue. She walked along Ninth Avenue to Elm Street and turned right. She walked up Elm Street to Eighth Avenue and turned right again. She went to a building on the left, between the flower shop and the post office.

2. Roger was at the shoe store on Eighth Avenue. He walked along Eighth Avenue to Oak Street and turned right. He walked down Oak Street and went to a building on the left, across from the parking garage.

3. Mr. and Mrs. Baker were at the book store on Elm Street. They walked up Elm Street to Eighth Avenue and turned right. They walked along Eighth Avenue to a building next to the pet shop and across from the post office.

4. Wanda was at the department store on Ninth Avenue. She walked along Ninth Avenue to Oak Street and turned left. She walked up Oak Street to a building on the right, next to the toy store and across from the library.

5. Alan was at the motel on Oak Street. He walked down Oak Street to Ninth Avenue and turned right. He walked along Ninth Avenue to a place on the left, next to the supermarket and across from the department store.

6. Alice was at the supermarket on Ninth Avenue. She walked along Ninth Avenue to Oak Street and turned left. She walked up Oak Street to Eighth Avenue and turned right. She went to a building on the left, across from the restaurant.

Page 67 Exercise I

Listen and fill in the correct places.

1. David took the Bay Avenue bus and got off at Second Street. He walked up Second Street to Brighton Boulevard and turned right. He walked along Brighton Boulevard to a building on the right, across from the post office. Where did he go?

2. Barbara took the Day Street bus and got off at Second Street. She walked down Second Street to Bay Avenue and turned right. She walked along Bay Avenue to a building between the flower shop and the church. Where did she go?

3. Mr. and Mrs. Jackson took the Bay Avenue bus and got off at First Street. They walked up First Street to Brighton Boulevard and turned left. They walked along Brighton Boulevard to a building on the right, next to the bus station and across from the barber shop. Where did they go?

4. Susan didn't want to take the bus this morning. She was at the library on Bay Avenue. She walked along Bay Avenue to Third Street and turned left. She walked up Third Street to Day Street and turned left again. She walked along Day Street and went to a building on the left, between First Street and Second Street. Where did she go?

5. Mr. and Mrs. Yamamoto wanted to get some exercise this morning. They took the Day Street bus and got off at First Street. They walked down First Street to Brighton Boulevard and turned left. They walked along Brighton Boulevard to Second Street and turned right. They walked down Second Street to Bay Avenue and turned right again. They went to a place on the right, at the corner of First Street and Bay Avenue, next to the concert hall. Where did they go?

6. George got lost this morning. He took the Bay Avenue bus and got off at First Street. He walked up First Street to Brighton Boulevard and turned right. He walked along Brighton Boulevard to Second Street and turned left. He walked up Second Street to Day Street and turned right. He walked along Day Street to Third Street and turned right again. He walked down Third Street to Brighton Boulevard, and then he was happy. He went to a place at the corner of Third Street and Brighton Boulevard, next to the post office and across from the pet shop. Where did he go?

Page 69 Exercise C

Listen and circle the correct word to complete the sentence.

1. He's a good worker, but he's . . .
2. She's an excellent violinist. She plays the violin . . .
3. I don't think he's an honest card player. To tell the truth, everybody says he's . . .
4. I can't read their homework because they write very . . .

5. Maria never makes mistakes. She's very . . .
6. Their son Marvin is very polite. He never speaks . . .
7. When you leave the party, please drive home . . .
8. Their car is very old. I don't think it's . . .
9. People can't hear you very well when you speak . . .
10. We never buy expensive clothes. We live very . . .
11. You rode your motorcycle carelessly yesterday. That's strange. You usually ride it very . . .
12. Everybody in the store likes Jane. She works hard, and when she talks to customers she's very . . .

Page 80 Exercise F

Listen and fill in the correct places.

1. Mrs. Mendoza was at the hotel at the corner of First Avenue and Grove Street. She walked up Grove Street to Second Avenue and turned left. She walked along Second Avenue to a building on the left, between the pet shop and the cafeteria. Where did she go?

2. Edward was at the football stadium on First Avenue. He walked along First Avenue to Elm Street and turned left. He walked up Elm Street to Second Avenue and turned right. He walked along Second Avenue to a building on the right, at the corner of Grove Street and Second Avenue, across from the bank. Where did he go?

3. Mr. and Mrs. Wong were at the post office on Second Avenue. They walked along Second Avenue to Grove Street and turned left. They walked down Grove Street to First Avenue and turned right. They went to a building on the left, across from the museum and the parking garage. Where did they go?

4. Thomas was at the hospital on Second Avenue. He walked along Second Avenue to Elm Street and turned right. He walked down Elm Street to First Avenue and turned left. He walked along First Avenue to a building on the left, at the corner of Grove Street and First Avenue, across from the supermarket. Where did he go?

5. Maria was at the shoe store on First Avenue. She walked along First Avenue to Grove Street and turned left. She walked up Grove Street to Second Avenue and turned left again. She walked along Second Avenue to a building on the right, between the toy store and the barber shop, across from the ice cream shop. Where did she go?

Page 83 Exercise E

Listen and choose the correct answer.

1. A. What was he doing yesterday when the lights went out?
   B. He was shaving.
2. A. What was she doing yesterday when you saw her?
   B. She was skating.
3. A. What were they doing when it started to rain?
   B. They were swimming at the beach.
4. A. What was he doing yesterday when you called?
   B. He was studying math.
5. A. What were you doing when your friends arrived?
   B. We were eating.
6. A. What was she doing when you saw her?
   B. She was talking with her mother.
7. A. What was he doing when you called?
   B. He was taking a shower.
8. A. What were you doing when the guests arrived?
   B. I was sweeping the living room.

Page 84 Exercise G

Listen and put the number under the correct picture.

1. I saw you yesterday at about 3:00. You were walking into the bank.
2. I saw you yesterday at about 1:30. You were jogging through the park.
3. I saw you yesterday at about 2:00. You were getting off the D Train.
4. I saw you yesterday at about 5:00. You were getting on the B Train.
5. I saw you yesterday at about 4:45. You were getting out of a taxi on Fifth Street.
6. I saw you yesterday at about noon. You were getting into a taxi on Sixth Street.
7. I saw you yesterday at about 11:45. You were getting on a bus.
8. I saw you yesterday at about 9:00. You were getting off a bus.

Page 88 Exercise M

Listen and choose the correct answer.

1. A. Why does Sally look so upset?
   B. She lost her new boot.
2. A. What happened to Howard?
   B. He burned himself while he was cooking.
3. A. When did you see them?
   B. While they were walking out of the park.
4. A. You look upset. What happened?
   B. Someone stole our new fan.

5. A. I had a bad day today.
   B. Why? What happened?
   A. I dropped my new CD player.
6. A. What happened to Charlie?
   B. A dog bit him while he was walking.
7. A. What were you doing when the accident happened?
   B. We were driving over a bridge.
8. A. What happened to Helen?
   B. She tripped and fell on the kitchen floor.
9. A. When did they drop their packages?
   B. While they were walking up the stairs.
10. A. What was Jane doing when she hurt herself?
    B. She was cooking on the barbecue.
11. A. You look upset. What's the matter?
    B. I cut myself while I was chopping.
12. A. What happened to Fred?
    B. He fainted at the bus stop.

Page 98 Exercise K

Listen to each story, and then choose the correct answers to the questions you hear.

William's New Apartment

William is having problems with his new apartment. Yesterday he was very frustrated. It was a hot day, and he wasn't able to open his living room windows. And today he's upset because all the lights in his apartment went out. William is very disappointed. Now he won't be able to cook dinner or watch his favorite programs on TV.

1. Why was William frustrated yesterday?
2. Why is he upset today?
3. Why is he disappointed?

Mr. and Mrs. Clark's New Computer

Mr. and Mrs. Clark are having problems with their new computer. Yesterday they were frustrated because they couldn't assemble the computer easily. And today they're upset because the computer crashed. Mr. and Mrs. Clark are very disappointed. Now they won't be able to send any e-mail to their grandchildren.

4. Why were Mr. and Mrs. Clark frustrated yesterday?
5. Why are they upset today?
6. Why are they disappointed?

Page 102 Exercise E

Listen to the story, and then choose the correct answers to the questions you hear.

Poor Janet!

Last year Janet's teacher said she couldn't dance in the school play because she was too clumsy. Janet was very upset. This year Janet practiced every day, and now she dances much better. Unfortunately, last week she fell down while she was dancing and she hurt herself. Janet is very disappointed. She won't be able to dance in the play this year.

1. Why was Janet upset last year?
2. What did Janet do this year?
3. What happened while Janet was dancing last week?
4. Why is Janet disappointed?

Page 109 Exercise J

Listen and choose the correct answer.

1. Mr. Lopez, I'm really worried about your eyes.
2. Mrs. Parker, I'm concerned about your heart.
3. I saw my doctor today, and she's concerned about my stomach.
4. Ms. Smith, I'm worried about your blood pressure.
5. Ricky, I'm concerned about your hearing.
6. I saw my doctor today, and he's concerned about my knees.

Page 115 Exercise E

Listen and choose the correct answer.

1. A. What will Betty be doing this afternoon?
   B. She'll be ironing dresses.
2. A. What will Sally and Tom be doing this morning?
   B. They'll be working downtown.
3. A. What will your husband be doing today?
   B. He'll be knitting on the front porch.
4. A. Will you be busy tonight?
   B. Yes, I will. I'll be watching sports.
5. A. Will you and Frank be busy in a half hour?
   B. Yes, we will. We'll be feeding the baby.
6. A. What will Charles be doing later tonight?
   B. He'll be taking a bath.
7. A. Will you and your husband be home this morning?
   B. Yes, we will. We'll be home all morning. We'll be baking cakes.
8. A. Will your daughter be busy this afternoon?
   B. Yes, she will. She'll be doing her homework.
9. A. What will Teddy and Timmy be doing this Sunday morning?
   B. I'm sure they'll be sleeping all morning.
10. A. Will your daughter be home this afternoon?
    B. No, she won't. She'll be skateboarding in the park.
11. A. Will you and your wife be busy this afternoon?
    B. Yes, we will. I think we'll be walking the dog.
12. A. I'm sad that you're leaving.
    B. I know. But don't worry. I'll be thinking about you all the time.

Page 122 Exercise E

Listen to each conversation, and then choose the correct answers to the questions you hear.

Conversation 1

A. I just found this brown wallet on my desk. Is it yours?

B. No. It isn't mine. But it might be John's. He lost his last Tuesday.

A. Thanks. I'll call him right away.

B. I hope it's his. He was very upset when he lost it.

   1. Where was the wallet?

   2. Is the wallet John's?

   3. When did John lose it?

Conversation 2

A. Hello, John? This is Jane. I just found a brown wallet on my desk at work. Is it yours?

B. No. Unfortunately, it isn't mine. Mine is black. But it might be Mary's. She lost hers, too.

A. Okay. I'll call her right away.

B. I hope it's hers. She was very upset when she lost it.

   4. What color is John's wallet?

   5. What did Mary lose at work?

   6. Is the wallet Mary's?

Page 126 Exercise H

Listen and choose the correct response.

1. How was the prom last Saturday?
2. How was your new tuxedo?
3. Was there any good music?
4. How late did you stay?
5. Why did you leave so early?
6. Do you think next year's prom will be better?

Page 129 Exercise L

Listen and choose the person you should call.

1. A. I'm having trouble with my new car!
   B. You should call . . .

2. A. There's water on my bathroom floor!
   B. You should call . . .

3. A. My keys won't open the door lock!
   B. You should call . . .

4. A. My upstairs neighbor lifts weights at two o'clock in the morning!
   B. You should call . . .

5. A. The lights in my kitchen won't go on!
   B. You should call . . .

6. A. Someone stole my bicycle!
   B. You should call . . .

7. A. I can't turn off my kitchen faucet!
   B. You should call . . .

8. A. My computer crashes every day!
   B. You should call . . .

Exercise D Page 133

Listen and choose the correct answers to complete the sentences.

1. Good morning. I'm Doctor Johnson. Today I'll be giving you. . .
2. First, you'll stand on a scale and the nurse will measure . . .
3. Next, the nurse will take your . . .
4. Then you'll go to the lab for some blood tests and . . .
5. Next, we'll go into the examination room and I'll look at your . . .

Correlation Key

STUDENT TEXT PAGES	ACTIVITY WORKBOOK PAGES	STUDENT TEXT PAGES	ACTIVITY WORKBOOK PAGES
Chapter 1		**Chapter 8**	
2	2	72	68–70
3	3	73	71
4-5	4–7	74	72–73
6	8	76	74–76
7	9–11	77	77
		79	78
Chapter 2			
12	12–13	**Check-Up Test**	**79–80**
13	14–15	**Chapter 9**	
14	16–17	84	81–83
15	18–20	85	84–85
		87	86
Chapter 3		88-89	87–90
20	21–23		
21	24	**Chapter 10**	
23	25–26	94	91–92
24	27	95	93
		96	94–95
Check-Up Test	**28–29**	98-99	96–97
Chapter 4		101	98–100
30	30		
31	31–33	**Check-Up Test**	**101–102**
33	34	**Chapter 11**	
34	35	106-107	103
35	36–39	108-109	104–106
		111	107–108
Chapter 5		112	109
40	40	113	110
41	41–42		
42-43	43–46	**Chapter 12**	
45	47–49	116	111
47	50	117-118	112–113
		119	114–115
Chapter 6		120	116
50	51	122	117–119
51	52–54		
54-55	55–57	**Chapter 13**	
		126	120
Check-Up Test	**58–59**	127	121
Chapter 7		128-129	122–124
62	60	130	125–126
63	61	131-132	127–131
64-65	62–64		
66	65–66	**Check-Up Test**	**132–133**
67	67		